An Economic Theory of Home Schooling

An Economic Theory of Home Schooling

Brian Baugus

LEXINGTON BOOKS
Lanham • Boulder • New York • London

Published by Lexington Books
An imprint of The Rowman & Littlefield Publishing Group, Inc.
4501 Forbes Boulevard, Suite 200, Lanham, Maryland 20706
www.rowman.com

6 Tinworth Street, London SE11 5AL, United Kingdom

Copyright © 2022 The Rowman & Littlefield Publishing Group, Inc.

All rights reserved. No part of this book may be reproduced in any form or by any electronic or mechanical means, including information storage and retrieval systems, without written permission from the publisher, except by a reviewer who may quote passages in a review.

British Library Cataloguing in Publication Information Available

Library of Congress Cataloging-in-Publication Data

Names: Baugus, Brian, author.
Title: An economic theory of home schooling / Brian Baugus.
Description: Lanham, Maryland : Lexington Books, 2022. | Includes bibliographical references and index. | Summary: "In this book, Brian Baugus examines home schooling as an education enterprise, arguing that successful home school families have the same characteristics and motivations as entrepreneurs"— Provided by publisher.
Identifiers: LCCN 2021056696 (print) | LCCN 2021056697 (ebook) | ISBN 9781793631749 (cloth) | ISBN 9781793631763 (paperback) | ISBN 9781793631756 (ebook)
Subjects: LCSH: Home schooling—Economic aspects—United States.
Classification: LCC LC40 .B24 2022 (print) | LCC LC40 (ebook) | DDC 371.04/2—dc23/eng/20211220
LC record available at https://lccn.loc.gov/2021056696
LC ebook record available at https://lccn.loc.gov/2021056697

Matthew 6:33

Contents

Acknowledgments		ix
1	A Brief History of Home Schooling in the United States	1
2	The Problem with the Public-School System	13
3	Entrepreneurship Theory and Its Application to the Home School Family	31
4	Entrepreneurship in Education: What Home Schools Do	49
5	Home School Investment and Profits	65
6	Leviathan Grows Restless	101
7	So What Happens Next?	121
Bibliography		125
Index		133
About the Author		139

Acknowledgments

This book was over a decade in the making. Not in the writing process but from the time I first became interested in applying entrepreneurial analysis to home schoolers until I finished the final chapter was fourteen years. The people that helped me along the way are too many to list and thank but know if you talked to me about home schooling or answered my questions or provided me any little insights and thoughts I am grateful.

However, there are some I do need to thank by name starting with my wife Ildiko. She was the first to introduce me to the idea of home schooling and we have spent a lot of time discussing it, and she provided invaluable insights and help throughout those fourteen years, as well as almost thirty years of marriage. There is no book without her. I also thank Dr. Richard Wagner at George Mason University who saw an early version of this as my doctoral dissertation and though it is much changed and updated for developments since then, it retains a core of that work that he helped me think about and strengthen.

I also want to thank the team from Rowman and Littlefield's Lexington Books for their patience and willingness to extend deadlines for when our house was partially destroyed and then for Covid-related issues. It was a struggle for all of us this last twenty-four months and their flexibility was vital. So, thank you Joe Parry and Alex Alexandra Rallo and your associates for sticking with this.

Finally, I want to thank the Institute for Humane Studies for their support. IHS provided some valuable research assistance and helped make this a better product than it would have been. They are great supporters of many academic projects and I am grateful they decided to support me from the plethora of options they have.

All of these and so many more made this book possible and better but ultimately I am responsible for its content, and any errors or omissions are solely mine.

To God Be the Glory

Chapter 1

A Brief History of Home Schooling in the United States

Home schooling, the provision of elementary and secondary education to a family's children, is considered a recent development in education, dating to the late 1960s in its earliest form. But, providing education at home is not new; it has been an approach used for literally thousands of years, and the reality is that the practice of the state being the primary provider of education is the newer idea. However, I have not written a history of home schooling, but no treatment and analysis is complete without discussing some key historical developments: it sets the context and establishes the perspective needed to fully appreciate the analysis.

Many of us are familiar with biographies about historically notable figures whose education either was entirely or mostly at home. However, starting in the mid-nineteenth century, states enacted compulsory attendance laws which were either written or interpreted in a way that made home schooling illegal. While home schooling was rare after the introduction of the public-school system, and reports of it even more so, we do get a glimpse of the reaction to early home school families. On November 3, 1936, *The New York Times* contained a story about Mr. and Mrs. Benno Bongart and family. Mrs. Bongart was on trial in Domestic Relations court in Newark, New Jersey, for home schooling her two sons, William and Robert. The Bongarts withdrew their children from the Washington public school in West Orange, New Jersey, when the principal corporally punished William. As a result, the Bongarts were charged with violating the 1903 truancy law. In court testimony William stated that in a year of home schooling he had surpassed his grade level in arithmetic, geography, music, current events, and history.[1]

There are other small news stories along the way with parents facing similar charges but it was not just the earlier years in which home schoolers ran afoul of state laws. Local boards of education and state departments of education regularly took home school parents to court on various charges including truancy, child abuse, operating an illegal school, teaching without a certification or license, and other violations well into the 1990s and it still happens on occasion. After court decisions began to favor parents, the state education establishments pushed new legislation to stop home schooling or at least limit it. The quantity and aggressiveness of these efforts have waned and may die out completely in the aftermath of the surge in home schooling and other innovative efforts due to the corona virus closing all schools of all types, but state efforts to control home schooling are not dead yet as is demonstrated in the recent ruling by California's Second District court that someone can only teach if they are state certified to teach in the subject area.[2] The politically powerful teachers' unions are still officially opposed to home schooling as this statement from the National Education Association's 2016–2017 Resolutions shows:

> The National Education Association believes that home schooling programs based on parental choice cannot provide the student with a comprehensive education experience. When home schooling occurs, students enrolled must meet all state curricular requirements, including the taking and passing of assessments to ensure adequate academic progress. Home schooling should be limited to the children of the immediate family, with all expenses being borne by the parents/guardians. Instruction should be by persons who are licensed by the appropriate state education licensure agency, and a curriculum approved by the state department of education should be used. The Association also believes that home schooled students should not participate in any extracurricular activities in the public-schools. The Association further believes that local public-school systems should have the authority to determine grade placement and/or credits earned toward graduation for students entering or re-entering the public-school setting from a home school setting.[3]

While this statement is not specifically against home schooling, if its recommendations were followed, all home schools would just be miniature replicas of the public schools, the exact opposite of what home school parents are trying to achieve.

IN THE BEGINNING...

The earliest home school parents were mostly members of counter-cultural groups. Challenges to the status quo are more likely to come from the margins of society which is why the idea of home schooling first emerged in the hippie community and later in the fundamentalist Christian community.[4]

With no end in sight to the war in Vietnam and the election of people like Nixon as president and Reagan as governor of California a certain element of society became disillusioned by their lack of progress in the political sphere and became increasingly inspired by certain kinds of alternative worldviews such as Timothy Leary's "turn on, tune in, drop out" mantra. While this phrase has become clichéd and a punch line over the years it is a concise description of a certain philosophy. As a result, hippies rejected many aspects of mainstream culture and home schooling was consistent with this approach to life. As Leary explained: "'Drop out' meant a voluntary detachment from involuntary commitments like school, the military, and corporate employment."[5]

Similar disillusionment with modern society was occurring among evangelical Christians. A society that was at least historically friendly to Christianity seemed to be moving in a new direction in the 1960s, with many changes including the abolition of prayer in public schools, a new more radical politics forming on college campuses; Western civilization in general and Christianity in particular seemed to be under attack and Christian thinkers like Francis Schaeffer and R. J. Rushdoony started addressing these social changes and the proper Christian response to them and education was at the heart of this conversation.

Schaeffer was a leading intellectual light in the Christian community, and education and culture were subjects he was very passionate about, having established Christian study center in Switzerland and authoring numerous books on Christian philosophy. As excerpts from this talk he gave in 1982 show, he was calling the Christian community to think differently about education:

> Now, moving from public-schools to private schools, what is the priority? Notice I am not saying Christian schools, but all private schools, including Christian schools. If you are really going to do something here, you have to think larger than your own interest. What we must do for the private schools, including the Christian schools, is to stand against those who have done so much to ruin our public-schools. We must not allow those who have ruined the public-schools to get a hold on the private schools, and specifically, the Christian schools, through a control of the curriculum. What we should be doing is struggling to see that the Christian school's curriculum is not controlled by those who have with their world view ruined the public-schools.
>
> We must say that we are going to control the curriculum. We are not going to let the state bring in the materialistic view as the final reality through the back door
>
> It is not just to be negative. It should be a superior education, if you are going to really protect the Christian school. It should certainly teach the students how

to read and write and how to do mathematics better than most public-schools are able to do today. It should do that but it should also appreciate and teach the full scope of human learning. Christian education is indeed knowing the Bible—of course it is—but Christian education should also deal with all human knowledge. We can think of what I said previously about the humanities. Christian education should deal with all human knowledge—presenting it in a framework of truth, rooted in the Creator's existence, and in his creation. Real Christian education, if we are going to protect our Christian schools, is not just the negative side, it is positive, touching on all human knowledge; and in each case, according to the level of the students, showing how it fits into the total framework of truth, the truth of all reality as rooted in the Creator's existence and in His creation. If the Judeo-Christian position is the truth of all reality (and it is!), then all the disciplines, and very much including a knowledge of, and I would repeat, an appreciation of, the humanities and the arts should be a part of Christian education.

True Christian education is not a negative thing; it is not a matter of isolating the student from the full scope of knowledge. Isolating the student from large sections of human knowledge is not the basis of a Christian education. Rather it is giving him or her the framework or total truth, rooted in the Creator's existence and in the Bible's teaching, so that in each step of the formal learning process the student will understand what is true and what is false and why it is true or false.

In short, Christian education should produce students more educated in the totality of knowledge, culture and life, than non-Christian education rooted in a false view of truth. The Christian education should end with a better educated boy and girl and man and woman, than the false could ever produce.[6]

This is a rather long excerpt but I wanted to present the significant challenges the serious Christian was considering at the time. Not only did this Christian philosopher explain why the public system was inadequate for Christians, he also explained that some Christian schools may be as well. This would leave only one option: home schooling.

WHY HIPPIES AND CHRISTIANS? A SOCIAL CONNECTIVITY THEORY OF HOME SCHOOLING'S ORIGINS

Upon first glance and even second glance, hippies and Christians would not seem to have very much in common; it could be said that hippies were in many ways re-acting to a culture and society that was, if not Christian, heavily influence by Christian teachings and thought. At the same time Christians were figuring out how to respond to a society that was quickly embracing some of the secular and alternate worldviews that the hippies favored. Society was a mix and meeting in the middle and it was leaving both of these groups marginalized into a subculture. To understand how important these subcultures were as incubators for home schooling, we need to look at the larger society first.

Models of Society

A society can be modeled as a series of nodes connected by relationships. These relationships have varying strengths. Some are relatively weak and temporary such as the relationship between a customer and a cashier at a store one seldom visits. Other relationships are stronger like the staff at a store one often visits, and some are very strong such as that between coworkers and church members, and finally the strongest relationships are those between friends and family. In a simple diagram a community could be represented as in figure 1.1.

In figure 1.1 the octagons represent independent nodes and the lines connecting them represent various relationships. The thickness of the line represents the strength of the relationships that connect the nodes. A family and public school are independent nodes but are connected through relationships such as compulsory attendance, parent-teacher associations, taxes, and sports events. Many of these relationships are weak, some are strong but there are many of them making the entire relationship strong and significant.

In any community there are pockets of smaller communities heavily connected between its own members. This is anything from a family to clubs and workplaces, and larger communities are full of subcommunities. However, if a subcommunity is or becomes a subculture, the nature and character of the group is different.

A subcommunity is a smaller group within the larger community connected through stronger relationships but is essentially a reflection of the larger community in beliefs and practices. A subculture is a subcommunity but differs in fundamental ways possibly in beliefs, practices, traditions, or in many other ways. A few prominent examples are some orthodox Jewish communities, the Amish, and first-generation immigrants from the same country. Hippies and certain flavors of American Christians were also subcultures. Subcultures may still be very connected to the larger community; people still shop and work and start business and go to the movies; not all choose to be as detached as the Amish, but subcultures are characterized as having strong connections in some significant ways to other members of the subculture, often at the cost of weaker connections to the larger community. The diagram would look more like figure 1.2.

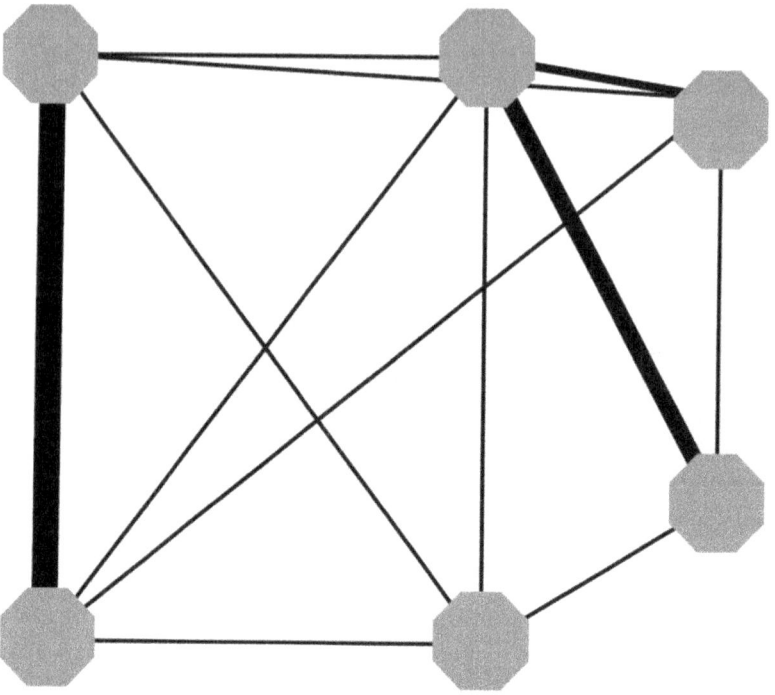

Figure 1.1 **Community as a Network of Nodes Connected by Relationships.** Created by Brian Baugus.

In figure 1.2, the octagons represent various mainstream entities and the circles represent members of a subculture. The connections people build within their networks are part of their *social capital*. Journalist, author, and pioneering urban studies researcher Jane Jacobs first coined the term "social capital" to describe the existence and development of networks within a community.[7] Robert Putnam in his book *Bowling Alone: The Collapse and Revival of American Community* expanded on Jacobs to describe inclusive and exclusive social capital.[8] Inclusive social capital is the development of an extensive system of weak relationships similar to figure 1.1, the "Informal networks and relationships that exist amongst any large group of people that in some way facilitate purposeful action."[9] Exclusive social capital "describes the cohesion that exists between small groups of similar people such as family members, close friends and colleagues and perhaps the members of ethnic or religious groups."[10]

People's accumulation of social capital is both incidental and purposeful. They build social capital through daily contacts and associations in just living their lives and interacting with other people. They also deliberately build

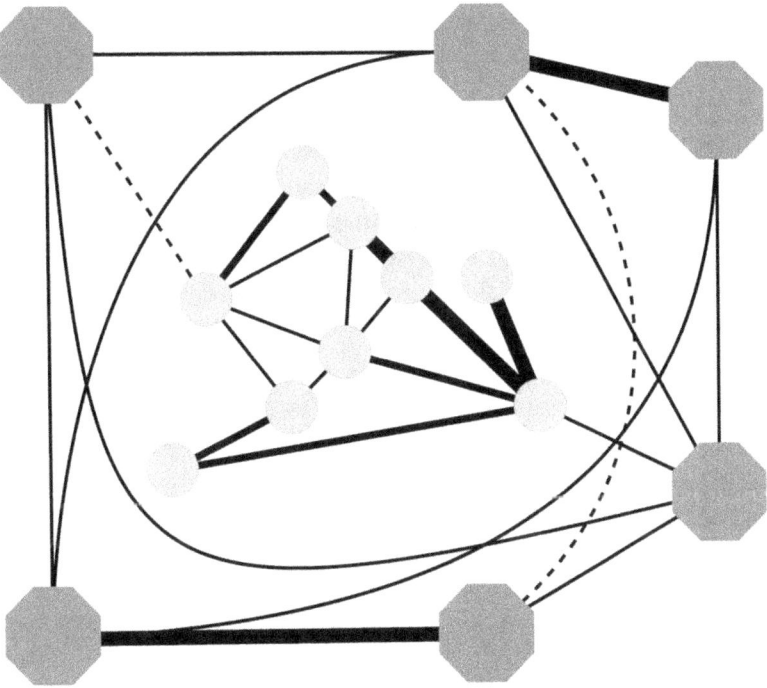

Figure 1.2 A Community with Subcultures. Created by Brian Baugus.

networks to achieve certain goals. People develop specific social capital with a purpose. Personal, social, political, and business relationships are established and nurtured over time and provide certain kinds of returns including social and professional acceptance and advancement. Acceptance and, for some, admiration by others within the community help facilitate the individual's ability to function within the community. We see this manifested in all sorts of ways: the new kid at school, the new family in the neighborhood, and the new person at work have to build their relationships, which will often determine how they are perceived and how their future dealings proceed. A highly connected person has a well-diversified social capital portfolio but is heavily invested in his inclusive form of social capital. It is costly to break or weaken those connections. This is exactly what would have been required for the home school movement to start among the culturally accepted. In the early years becoming a home school family could be isolating and required the sacrifice of accumulated and potential social capital developed from school connections lost or never made. The public school is one of those dominating nodes; many relationships and much of life are dictated and built around the daily and annual school schedule. Furthermore, and maybe more importantly, if both spouses worked there were also lost professional connections as one parent became a stay-at-home teacher. These are not small considerations.

While home schooling is now more accepted and more widely practiced, in the early years it was a significant change from the norm. "Home schooling families are, however, breaking a pattern established since colonial times—education has been becoming increasingly institutionalized, formal, and removed from the family."[11] Thinking about this reality and comparing figures 1.1 and 1.2 we can see that breaking established patterns is a lower-cost choice for subcultures that have already broken with other aspects of society and are more reliant on exclusive social capital rather than inclusive. Early home school parents from both subculture groups invested in their exclusive social capital and were not as dependent on inclusive social capital and may have gained status within their subculture by not having their children immersed in a culture they had rejected. However, home schooling eventually spread out from the subculture groups.

Public success, such as home school children winning spelling and geography bees, attracted attention from parents outside the original subculture networks who were nonetheless dissatisfied with the public-school system. There were other dissatisfied parents looking for a solution but "[T]o take advantage of available opportunities one must first perceive them. To 'learn' free information one must perceive the opportunity to do so."[12] Public successes were a signal to other parents who then became aware of an alternative education approach and saw it for the first time as a viable option and this free information created many entrepreneurial moments, such as this story demonstrates:

> When Penny Wayne-Shapiro first let it slip to her friends that she was thinking of home schooling her son, then just a toddler, the idea drew plenty of raised eyebrows and blank stares. But nowadays, people don't bat an eye when she tells them she's turning her back on the highly regarded public-schools in her area to home school Ben, now 4, after he finishes preschool. Once stereotyped as a fringe movement for libertarians, religious extremists, or New Age nonconformists, home schooling is progressively elbowing its way into the mainstream. "It's normal people now, not just left-wing hippies or right-wing fundamentalists," Wayne-Shapiro said. "It's your neighbor down the block or your friend across town. There's a whole community around this, and there's strength in numbers."[13]

This quote from an article dated December 28, 2003, issue of the *Boston Globe* sums up the early history concisely; home schooling was in subcultures and when mainstream people discussed it there was already some social capital at risk as one can tell by her friends' skeptical reactions. But, after success and wider acceptance, others began and felt more comfortable pursuing this option.

More Public Success: The Colfax Brothers

One of those public successes was the Colfax family. It is one thing to win spelling bees which is a great accomplishment but also possibly the result of special talent and focused practice, but consistent and repeated success is another thing altogether. The Colfax family were an example of just that. While not the first home school family they may have been the first prominent home school family, notable for their high-level success and for the book they wrote about it in 1988, *Home Schooling for Excellence*, that became something of a "how to" guide for many early home school families.

David and Micki Colfax and family lived on a remote ranch in California where the logistics of getting their four boys to the nearest public school were formidable. So, home schooling just became a natural choice, which may be one of the reasons they are such a powerful example, despite all the intellectual criticisms of public schools from the left and the right, for the Colfaxes home schooling was just a practical decision. They were not activists in any sense they just found the best solution to educating their children given the circumstances. The Colfaxes modeled much of what is necessary for home school success, lots of interest driven activities with the children working at their own pace. For example, the oldest son, Grant, did not start reading until he was nine years old. Also, there is an education philosophy that seems common to many home school families that a young Grant summed up accurately if a little ineloquently: "All [public] school is about is controlling children, teaching them what rank they fall in society, teaching them to obey orders. For the people at the top of the ladder, the school system works. That's why they're at the top. But it destroys a lot of kids' inherent creativity."[14] This is a theme echoed by other home school advocates such as John Taylor Gatto, the New York Teacher of the Year, who, coincidentally, resigned just a few months after Grant was interviewed, in a very public way (in *The Wall Street Journal* editorial page) citing, among other things, the creativity stifling nature of public schools. Grant goes on to offer rejoinders to some of the criticisms and challenges to home schoolers, before they were ever levied:

> A lot of home schoolers play school in their house. I don't think having a blackboard in the kitchen and teaching your kids how to read that way is very productive.... The worst thing that you can do is want to home school so that you can have more control over your child's life. You should view home schooling as a way of the child gaining control of his or her own life.[15]

Grant Colfax and two of his brothers, Drew and Reed, caused a small media sensation when they were admitted to and subsequently graduated from Harvard University in 1987, 1990, and 1992 respectively. Fourth son Garth did not go the Harvard route but was successful. As it turned out, the Colfaxes were at the beginning of a small but growing trend of home school graduates seeking college admission. In a 1989 article in the *Harvard Crimson* about the Colfax family, the Harvard dean of Admissions, William Fitzsimmons, reported that his office received applications from five to ten home school students each year, but had a favorable opinion of them.[16] By 2006, the *Crimson* reported that the admissions office received 100–200 applications from home school graduates each year.[17]

Grant was a Fulbright scholar and went on to earn his MD from Harvard as well and is an infectious disease expert who has advised presidents and served as President Obama's director of the Office of National AIDS Policy. Drew got a JD from the University of Michigan and an MD from Harvard (not to be outdone by his big brother, you little brothers reading this know what I mean) and Reed (who, along with Garth is an adopted son, is African American while Garth is Native American) got his JD from Yale and is a named partner at the Washington, DC, law firm Relman Colfax and specializes in civil rights litigation.

Why Some and Not Others?

Answering this question in detail is what this book is about, the answer lies in the fact that those who choose to home school, especially the early pioneers, were not just dissatisfied with public school, after all many people say they are dissatisfied with the public-school system. Also, being in a marginalized subculture was a necessary but not sufficient condition to become a home schooler, many in the subculture did not choose home schooling. The difference between dissatisfaction and becoming a home schooler is entrepreneurship.

This exploration analyzes home schoolers as entrepreneurs explaining that successful home school families have the same characteristics and motivations as entrepreneurs, of which dissatisfaction with the current offerings is only the beginning. As entrepreneurs, they consider costs and benefits or profits and have made rational decisions to invest in this enterprise and along the way have faced resistance from the established providers. Home schooling is an entrepreneurship story similar to any new technology or process that has come along and seeing it that way allows us to understand it more fully.

The choice to home school is, at its heart, a choice to begin production; to start an education enterprise. It is regularly said that education is an investment in the future and home schoolers (education entrepreneurs) are acting in accordance with this idea. It is a statement of action that claims that the well-financed, long-established, professionally run schools are producing inferior returns on the investment and that there are better options. That instead of relying on the socialized investment of taxes and government programs, investing privately, incurring risks, and seeking superior returns will provide their children with either a quantity of human capital or a quality of human capital or both that is customized and flexible and easily adaptable and, in some sense, better than the options already available. Based on superior knowledge a parent has of his or her child, parents provide an education tailored to the child, something the public schools just cannot do. I explore this in great detail in the following chapters and hopefully provide a new way to understand this growing, especially in a Covid and post-Covid world, movement.

WHAT THIS BOOK DOES FROM HERE

This book is motivated by the desire to explain why people choose to home school and offers a theory on how the successful ones get that way. Many studies of home schooling have focused on demographic issues and academic performance. These studies are useful and important but do not provide in-depth answers about why people home school which often concludes with some version of "the parents do not like public schools for some reason, probably religious." This leads to criticisms and conclusions that are largely unfounded and frequently seem to be based on stereotypes and biases based on faulty assumptions.

Many other studies make no attempt to discern why some dissatisfied parents choose to home school while others, who are demographically very similar, do not. There are some studies that assert home schooling is bad for the children and bad for society but must acknowledge home school students outperform public-school students and often private-school students as well. In short, many of the studies that purport to be rigorously critical and analytical are not.

This book offers a different perspective. I analyze the dissatisfaction many parents have, show how entrepreneurship theory explains home schoolers, then examine the costs and benefits, look at the resistance and criticisms, and speculate what might be next.

NOTES

1. Boy Backs Mother in Education Row 1936.

2. Jonathan L. et al. v. Los Angeles County Department of Children and Family Services et al. 2008.

3. National Education Association 2017.

4. Both "hippie" and "fundamentalist Christian" have become pejorative terms to many people. This adds support that these are subculture groups. I use the terms since they are known. By hippie I mean people who reject the established culture and frequently advocate ideas that may be broadly classified as libertarian left on the political spectrum. By evangelical or fundamentalist Christians, I mean people, usually of a Protestant denomination, who believe the Bible is the inerrant word of God and live their lives by its teachings and are frequently conservative on the political spectrum.

5. Leary, Flashbacks 1983, 253.

6. Schaeffer 1982.

7. Jacobs 1961, 138.

8. Putnam 2000.

9. Meadowcroft and Pennington Bonding and bridging: Social capital and the communitarian critique of liberal markets 2008, 121.

10. Meadowcroft and Pennington 2008, 122.

11. Hill Home Schooling and the Future of Public Education 2000, 21.

12. Kirzner, Competition and Entrepreneurship 1973, 227.

13. Schworn 2003.

14. Walters 1991.

15. Walters 1991.

16. Nahm 1989.

17. Pollack 2006.

Chapter 2

The Problem with the Public-School System

Everyone is at least a little dissatisfied with the public-school system but most like it well enough to support it. As one home school critic and public-school supporter, Professor T. Jameson Brewer, has said: "Public-schools are, by definition, artifacts of a societal obligation to fully socialize all children, and that entails engaging them in the full range of viewpoints and experiences that characterize a pluralistic, democratic society."[1] But Brewer's objections to home schooling are "not an endorsement of the current status in public-schools." He acknowledges that "there are serious issues and concerns," such as inequities in the system and problems with overcrowding and unfair practices. But he also expressed concern that "an increasing population of parents who are the most capable of helping to address those concerns—due to their relative wealth, education attainment, and other demographic advantages—are the ones who often opt for homeschooling."[2] In this article, literally within a few paragraphs Brewer calls home school parents anti-intellectual religious conservatives who want to indoctrinate their children *and* the very people who can fix public schools.[3] Such is the odd and schizophrenic thinking of many home schooling critics.

While some may have very differing views of home schooling, the American public has the same issue with public schools. This starts with the fact that the public-school system is a government creation. Few question the desirability of schools and educating the young. Public school is the government solution to this question but as with many government programs there are many and varied parties interested in the outcome. And they do not all agree as to what those outcomes should be. This means that government solutions, including public schools, are designed or, if not, soon morph into a compromise solution that tries to balance the desires and goals of these competing interests. These interest groups compete for budget and control and influence, and policy makers are caught between them. This inevitable compromise leaves most people involved a little dissatisfied but generally supportive but it does leave some very dissatisfied.

TWO VIEWS OF THE PUBLIC-SCHOOL SYSTEM

Essentially, and this is admittedly a little simplified, there are two views of the public-school system. One sees the public-school system as the great leveling ground of America, similar to what Professor Brewer stated in the previous paragraphs. It is where the wealthy meet the poor, black meets white, management meets labor, and so forth, while delivering a reasonably good education. This idealized view is reflected in popular culture, scanning the entertainment landscape of shows and stories set in high school we have seen this sort of portrayal for decades. The successful high-school entertainment offering always includes representatives of all the major high-school groups: athletes and nerds, good kids and bad kids, studious kids and slackers, and in more recent years broader racial and gender representation. *Archie Comics, Happy Days, Grease, Glee, High School Musical, Breakfast Club* all follow a certain formula that reflects this idealistic notion of what public schools are and do. Few, if any, think this is a perfectly accurate representation of the public system, even the strongest public school advocates acknowledge the systems' shortcomings, but this is the ideal, the goal for which the system strives.

But there is another way to view the school system. Some see the public school more like large mass production factories, basically providing standardized education with limited variation and not much room for diversity and creativity. To these parents, the public-school system is a significant misallocation of resources, failing to provide for their children in important ways. They want their child to get a customized education and the public school turns out a mass-produced product. We see this represented in the powerful documentary *Waiting for Superman* and the heartbreak of those who fail to get selected to leave their assigned public school and the elation of those who do get selected to go to one of the charter schools. These parents are trying to seize whatever opportunity they can find for improvement. They see that the school system's mass production one-size-fits-all public good approach to education is the exact opposite of the individualized private good they seek.

Home Schoolers: Can't Get No Satisfaction

The decision to home school starts with dissatisfaction emanating from the second view described earlier. Home schoolers may be a minority within that second group though as many parents will seek alternatives to public school like charter, magnet, and private schools. That is the point that so many critics miss, while some families may fall into home schooling as a sort of last option, successful home schooling is a choice that rejects not only the public-school system but the basic school model. Maybe the most tangible representations of the public-school model are bells and lines, not unlike old style factories, but the more significant aspect of the public-school model includes age-segregated classes that meet for a set amount of time each day and move students through a subject at the same pace, not unlike an assembly line. Making this even worse is the fact that there has been significant school consolidation:

> During most of the last century, the trend of consolidating small schools brought declines in the total number of public-schools in the United States. In 1929–30, there were approximately 248,000 public-schools, compared with about 98,000 in 2015–16. However, the number of public-schools has increased in recent decades: Between 1988–89 and 2006–07, there was an increase of approximately 15,600 schools. Since 2006–07, the number of public-schools has remained relatively stable, varying by fewer than 500 schools from year to year.[4]

A 60 percent decrease in the number of schools, over the years, despite a small increase lately, means that one size had to fit even more students than before. This development is also a recipe for larger frustration levels with its outcomes. Home schools are rejecting this model completely.

So, the analysis must begin here: home schooling is a choice, not a default setting for those with no other option as some imply, although Covid-19 may cause some to fall into home schooling by default. Those who sort of stumble into home schooling because they see it as the only option are more like the prevailing stereotype of people trying to recreate public school at home and many will struggle mightily. At this point I need to make a clarifying statement. I am examining successful home schooling, home schooling that accomplishes the parent and student goals. I will address some reasons for failure and criticisms, but the model I use here is an entrepreneurship model. In a parallel analogy, more than half of new businesses fail, we should expect failure in home schooling as well, and as with businesses the reasons for those failures are many. Educating children and even adults is difficult and requires hard trade-offs. After all, the public schools, with all its resources and professional experts, fail to educate an alarming number of its students: "More than 30 million adults in the United States cannot read, write, or do basic math above a third-grade level."[5] The search is not for the perfect education solution but for an approach for which the trade-offs make the most sense for any particular family; the

United States has a diverse student body, and it only makes sense that it also needs a diverse set of education options.

However, it cannot and should not be ignored that the public-school system is well supported and liked by many and not just because of the Hollywood ideal, but because it provides significant benefits to several politically powerful interest groups. The public-school system provides a basic education and, in some cases, a very good education. And, with its socialized costs, this is a very good deal for many families. It offers a set of trade-offs that many like or find least objectionable. The public-school system is a well-financed government agency, typically consuming a third to half of any local jurisdiction's annual budget with a significant federal component. But at its core, the public-school system is a political entity and this has several implications.

The Political Nature of Public Schools

The public-school system has been in existence in the United States in some form since the 1850s. It has grown from its early start in New England to become a large, centralized, bureaucratic organization in each state (with a federal layer as well) that is protected by compulsory attendance laws and financed by the state's ability to tax. Given these conditions it is very likely that almost every American has or will interact with the public-school system, either as an attendee, a taxpayer, or both.

Despite the coercive nature of the school system, it has a large number of supporters and like all institutions has an incentive to satisfy its benefactors. There are many politically powerful stakeholders that have an interest in the system and need to be satisfied by the system. Satisfying these groups is tricky business; they have an array of interests some which overlap but many that do not and all of these must be balanced to have a widely supported, stable institution.

Interest Groups Examined

Space limitations and focus preclude a detailed examination of every interest group involved in the public-school system; that could be a book unto itself but a review of a few interest groups and the dynamics involved illustrate the point.

Teachers' unions are possibly the best organized and most powerful interest group in the education establishment. They have strong interest in the outcome since they capture many benefits and bear many of the costs of any policy change. They are naturally organized around their private economic interests and desire the same thing all workers desire: higher wages, better working conditions, more say in management decisions, and to generally feel like their work matters and they are respected. There should be no doubt that teachers want to deliver a quality education but they want a number of other benefits as well and so they face certain trade-offs between their competing goals.

Parents are another interest group. They are not as well organized as teachers, hardly organized at all in most cases, but larger in number and more internally diverse. They have different incentives than teachers and many differing goals. Parents, and their children, are capturing large concentrated benefits at significantly smaller personal costs, but the benefits are a different set of benefits than the teachers. Parents want high-education quality and a large quantity and variety of other benefits, in a phrase they want it all for their children, academics, arts, sports, technology, social events, and more. Parents, as indirect employers of the teachers, want to work the teachers (and administrators and staffs) as hard and as long as they can to get "it all" for the children. It is only natural as parents and as consumers who are getting a lot of value at low personal cost to try to capture all the benefits possible.

The largest, least organized, and most diverse group are non-parent taxpayers which have a different set of incentives from either of the other two groups discussed. They are paying more costs and capturing the least direct benefits from the system although they may have in the past or will in the future. They want their money to be well spent but since they are not direct beneficiaries of the education, they have a demand for different benefits than parents. The government school system has become a vehicle for delivering a variety of non-educational goods and services. One study shows that "Ninety-five percent [of the public] believe schools should teach honesty . . . 80% believe they should be taught that girls can succeed at anything boys can . . . 61% advocate teaching respect for people who are homosexual."[6] Each person can decide if these particular goals are worthy or not, that is a different debate, but they are not part of what has traditionally been considered a basic education, the "three R's" as it was sometimes known. These and similar goals could be thought of as "good society" goals and are achieved at a cost. The public does seem to want those basic skills taught (and learned); as the article also points out, "The primary concerns about schools are the need for improved safety and a return to a basic skills emphasis."[7] But the public also expects the school system to deliver a variety of other benefits such as a good reputation of the neighborhood school system for the positive impact on property values, entertainment such as sporting and arts events, and so forth. It is a very large and mixed bag.

There are many more interest groups with an interest in the public-school system but the three briefly profiled here provide some insight into the

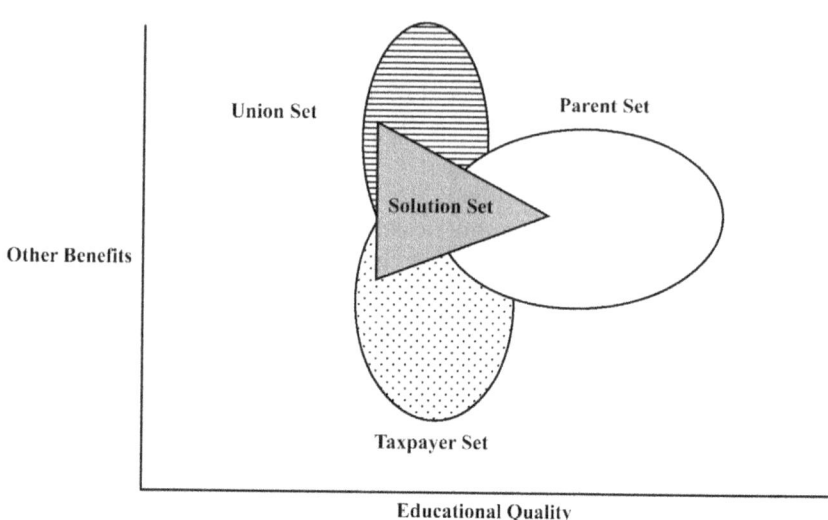

Figure 2.1 **The Solution Set for Educational Services.** Created by Brian Baugus.

political balancing act that is the public-school system, an act that can be shown graphically as in figure 2.1.

Each group's preferred solution set for school policy is represented by a different oval. The ovals' size represents the fact that, while the member of the group generally has the same preferences, there is some diversity within the group. Each oval occupies a certain position and direction representing the groups' general preferences and constraints. For example, the teachers' set shows that the teachers' desire to have a certain minimal level of educational quality but have a strong demand for other benefits such as better working conditions and higher pay and are willing to trade off some educational quality to obtain these benefits. However, they vary among themselves, hence the oval (compared to a dot if all teachers' preferences were identical) and are constrained by various realities such as the budget constraints and reactions of other interest groups.

The parents' set shows a greater diversity of views as one would expect from a larger and less organized group; some parents are highly focused on academics, some may be more focused on sports or arts, and so the set is larger, but in general all parents desire more of everything and, while still constrained in several ways, are less concerned about the constraints and costs since most of them are socialized. Non-parent taxpayers desire some minimal level of education but do not demand other benefits as much as the other groups do and also have different trade-offs and in some ways are one of the larger constraints on the other groups in that there is a limit to how much they are willing to pay.

So Much Pressure but So Much Stability: The Median Education

These preferences and constraints create pressure to provide a combination of education quality and other benefits that satisfy each group. The only viable policy solution is one where the various groups' interests coincide, that is the trade-offs each face is tolerable from their own perspective. This is represented by the triangle in the figure, which is the political solution set and much smaller than any of the ovals on the figure but if I were to add in other interest groups such as administrators, textbook and curriculum providers, and the federal education bureaucracy, as they are in real life, the figure would have ovals everywhere and the political solution set would be much smaller. However, even this limited example demonstrates how precarious this political balancing act truly is.

It would be reasonable to expect that competition between these interest groups would result in frequent and sometime messy policy disputes. In theory, a stable policy solution should not exist since interest groups exert multiple and competing pressures on the political process. The tendency would be for education policy to be unstable as the relative political power of the interest groups shift and we do see this at time with teachers' strikes and taxpayer revolts such as limiting property tax (the main funding source for public schools in most jurisdictions). But for the most part the system is very stable. The political solution set is in essence a bargain, an agreement between the interest groups. In a sense the political process here is to form a coalition between enough members of the various interest groups to create a policy solution that is stable and supported. This often means dividing the members of each group from other members of the group; the parent or teacher or anyone else at the fringe of their respective preference set are, to some extent, abandoned in favor of forming a coalition to create a workable policy solution.

The results of this workable policy solution have the advantage of being stable, and the supporters are committed to maintaining it, because of course it is providing some important benefits they desire. This creates long-term policy stability but tends to be inefficient. The pioneering Public Choice scholar Gordon Tullock (1981) described this as a form of logrolling and that

> the individual participants are well advised to sell out permanently rather than simply renting their vote. If they make it a practice of voting for some project and then after they have been paid off and then vote for its repeal, they will shortly find their vote is valued at very little by potential partners... we find that logrolling leads to two situations which are stable (in the sense of being unlikely to change) but non-Pareto optimal.[8]

Tullock is discussing voting in a legislature but it applies to any political process that requires balancing differing interests to get a single solution or outcome. In education, the public-school system is an outcome that can be described as a median education. An exact definition of a median education is not necessary and probably not possible although I think a strong definition would be a stable education solution that attempts to balance the demands of competing interest groups. But, there is some room in that solution set for variation, but not much.

While a form of logrolling explains how a solution emerges, its long-term stability comes from policies and practices like multi-year staggered terms of office for education policy makers, long-term contracts with both unions and material suppliers, educational policy decisions that are binding for several periods, and multiple layers of decision-making. These stability creating methods immunize the system and solution from temporary political shifts and exogenous shocks which is why politicians so rarely actually deliver on education reform regardless of how vigorous they may campaign for it or the voters may truly want it. In addition to the institutional stability of the education solution set there is interest group competition which counter-balances each other. If one group wants a change that another group opposes, that is probably enough to stop the change. The median solution creates a strong *status quo* bias in the system, which is not unique to the education system, it is throughout representative governments and frequently serves a positive purpose, it is hard for the government to surprise the people with some policy change, the Founders wanted to be sure that no one had enough power to make the government act quickly, change is normally slow. But that also means that the median education solution holds well and it is very difficult; it is not too strong to say impossible for a small disorganized group like a subset of frustrated parents to make meaningful impact on the school system. As Tullock says, "Consider an individual member or a small clique in such a coalition. In both cases assume defection would convert the majority into a minority coalition. For this individual or clique, there is no great advantage in being members of the existing coalition."[9] These folks, for whom there is no advantage of being in the coalition, is where all the action lies.

So, Is Everybody (Sort of) Happy?

In a word, no. Few people are truly happy with a median education because few are truly at the median, and most are dispersed throughout their interest groups' oval. The median education can work well if people are clustered around the median. As an example, some people in the United States point to the Nordic nations as models of what can be. It is true that some of the Nordic countries regularly appear in the top five of various studies of the world's best education systems, and Finland is consistently ranked number one.[10] Twenty years ago a 2000 report by the Paris-based Organization for Economic Cooperation and Development addressed the superiority of Finnish students: "In most countries, education feels like a car factory. In Finland, the teachers are the entrepreneurs."[11] This is highly instructive but this observation seems to be ignored by many. The finding in Finland is that schools are less like factories and are re-imagined by entrepreneurs. I will return to this very important idea. There are many people and studies researching why Finland consistently does so well, and I have seen a range of explanation and maybe the most absurd is that Finland is socialist, which it is not: "Finland has a highly industrialized, largely free-market economy with per capita GDP almost as high as that of Austria and the Netherlands and slightly above that of Germany and Belgium."[12] What Finland is is a very homogenous small population with a very entrepreneurial approach to education; by culture and policy choice it has a strong combination of positive factors in its approach to education. That is not necessarily a good model for a large diverse nation, unless that nation wants to break its system up into smaller units, like home schooling and its derivations (I will discuss co-ops in a later chapter). In fact, the four Nordic nations combined would only be the third most populous state, Sweden, the most populous would be the tenth most populous state and the others would be in the middle around the size of South Carolina or, appropriately enough Minnesota, but with much less diversity. South Carolina has three minority groups larger than any minority group in any Nordic country. Small and homogenous may not be a good model for a large and diverse nation but it does result in political solutions, including in education, that are extremely stable and widely supported. In a standard statistical graph, we can represent such a population in which the median education approach will result in minimum dissatisfaction with a population clustered around the median with very thin tails and highly peaked as seen in figure 2.2 with demographic diversity measured along the X-axis but with diversity measured as distance in either direction from the median, the X-axis does not increase from zero to positive infinity as one moves rightward along it. Zero diversity is measured as everyone being at the median and any deviation from the median represents greater diversity. Figure 2.2 shows nineteenth-century America or the Nordic countries or any of a number of countries that are highly homogenous.

"Despite the apparent simplicity of Finnish education, it would be tough to replicate in the U.S. With a largely homogeneous population, teachers have few students who don't speak Finnish. In the U.S. about 8% of students are learning English."[13] Some other examples between the United States and Finland help explain why the approach works well in Finland and not (as a system) in the United States:

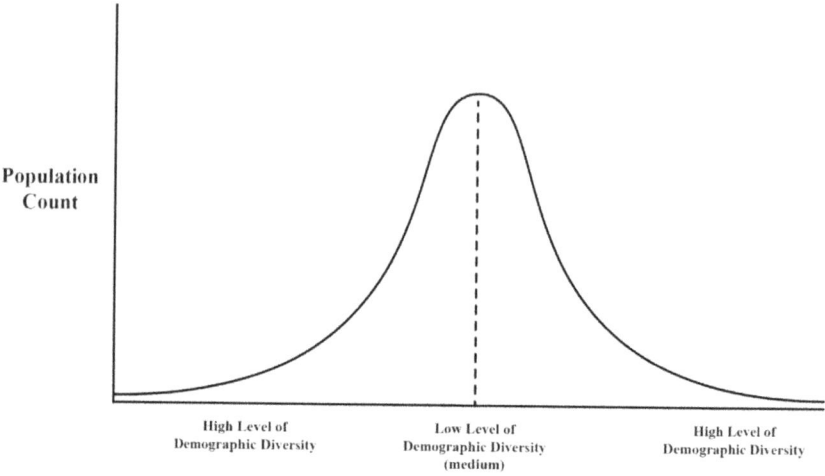

Figure 2.2 Population Distribution for Which a Median Education Would Be Acceptable. Created by Brian Baugus.

- Finland has 5.5 million citizens.
- In Finland almost 93 percent of the people speak one of the two official languages.
- The United States does not have an official language and only 78.2 percent speak the dominant language.
- In Finland 69.8 percent are Lutheran—a specific denomination within Protestant Christianity.
- In the United States 46.5 percent are Protestant which includes dozens of denominations.
- Finland has six very specifically defined ethnic groups large enough to register: Finn, Swede, Russian, Estonian, Romani, and Sami.
- The Unites States has six very broad ethnic group with dozens of subdivisions: white, black, Asian, Amerindian and Alaska native, native Pacific Islander, and bi-racial—these groupings lump Latin/Hispanic Americans (16.3 percent of the population) as one group despite representing dozens of countries and lumps them in with one or more of the other groups.[14]

Many educational professionals look to the Nordic model for ways to improve the U.S. public schools; they dismiss the significant factors of the extremely different populations and cultural characteristics and ignore many of the factors that the Finnish system have in common with home schooling: "[T]hey (Finland) have no school uniforms, no honor societies, no valedictorians, no tardy bells, and no classes for the gifted. There is little standardized testing and kids don't start school until age 7."[15] Also since the mid-1990s

Finland has had parental school choice[16] which implies that even in highly rated Finland there is some parental dissatisfaction.[17] It is just inherent in any government system no matter how good.

So, for a place like Finland, the solution set in figure 2.1 includes large portions of the various interest group ovals since the ovals themselves overlap. The highly homogenous culture and entrepreneurial approach lead to high (although not perfect) satisfaction rates. But in the United States with much more diversity in every way, the ovals are large and thick and there are relatively few whose preferred outcome is actually within the triangular solution set. The further any individual's preferred outcome is from the median, the greater the dissatisfaction. In a more complex model, with more interest groups represented and where the other benefits could be expanded into multiple dimensions, the median becomes very narrow and the solution set quite small, which makes the entire system inflexible and slow to adapt to change and accommodate exceptions. There is just not that much policy space for innovation and Finnish or home school type education entrepreneurship.

Late twentieth- or twenty-first-century American population is not clustered around the median and tends to have what statisticians call thick tails and is not usually well described by a mean or a median. A more accurate picture of the population distribution in modern America and other immigrant-friendly countries is presented in figure 2.3. It has the same measures and scales on the axis as figure 2.2 but with the thick tails representing much more heterogeneity within the population and with less clustering around a median.

As any statistician will tell you, the most interesting things in any distribution is in the tails. The tails are where Tullock's cliques are and where the most dissatisfied are and where the home schoolers are.

A View from the Tails

Demographic diversity means there will be high levels of dissatisfaction with a median education. But dissatisfaction runs on a scale.

Many parents and students are satisfied with the government-financed school; their preferred outcome is at or near the median, and these people are represented by the shaded area in figure 2.4. Some parents are mildly dissatisfied; they would like some changes at the margins but are not upset enough to abandon the public-school system; the socialized costs compensate them enough for their dissatisfaction. The parents may engage in some supplemental education activities such as family field trips or private lessons of one kind or another but they are on the whole more satisfied than dissatisfied. These people are represented in figure 2.4 between lines A and B but outside the shaded area. Some of the families on the edges of this range may

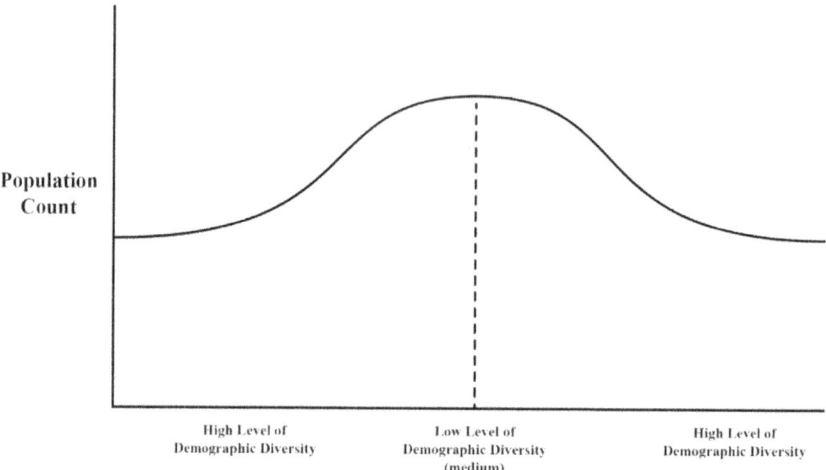

Figure 2.3 A Realistic Population Distribution for Which a Median Education Would Be Less Satisfactory. Created by Brian Baugus.

take more action. Evidence for this is suggested by the strong demand for the few specialized public schools that do exist such as charter schools and magnet school. There are slightly less than 4,000 charter schools and approximately 3,000 magnet and theme-based schools in the United States enrolling approximately 1 million students.[18] These numbers show a demand for choice but still within the public-school system.

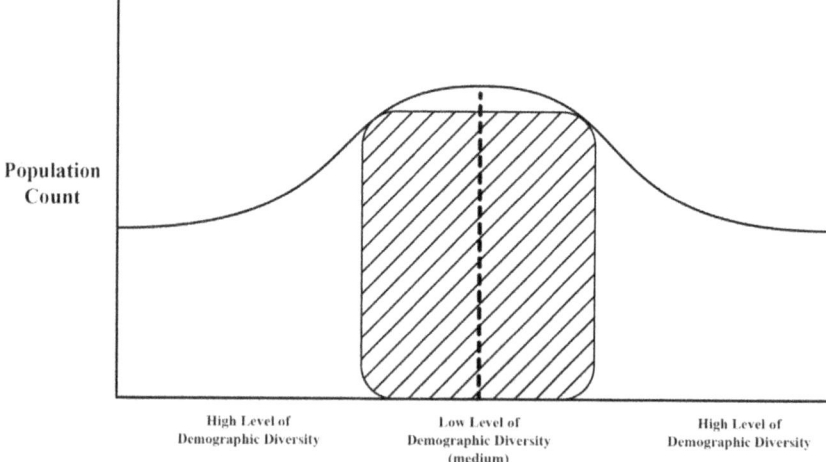

Figure 2.4 Measure of Satisfaction with the Government School. Created by Brian Baugus.

This dissatisfaction has been verified by various researchers (Garcia 2008, Holland 2007, West, Peterson, and Campbell 2001). One such report conducted for the U.S. Department of Education called the National Household Education Surveys Program (2003) points this fact out vividly. Table 2.1 reports some of the findings of this survey.

Based on the U.S. Department of Education's own research the shaded section in figure 2.4 represents 50 to 65 percent of public-school parents depending on the particular circumstances and exact factor being surveyed. Although not reproduced here, the survey from which table 2.1 is developed is much more in-depth and goes on to quantify all the regions in figure 2.4. The results have been pretty steady since 1993 for all categories over the fourteen years covered by the survey. The survey also shows, just looking at the most recent year, 2007, that of the parents of children in an assigned public school:

- 35 percent were somewhat satisfied,
- 8 percent were somewhat dissatisfied, and
- 5 percent were very dissatisfied.[19]

These results match up to figure 2.4 with 35 percent being between line A and line B; 8 percent being close to and on either side of lines A and B; and 5 percent being in the tails. Another consistency over time is that choice, any choice, even choice of another public school, improves satisfaction.

Other research supports the conclusion that many are dissatisfied with the public-school system. Rose and Gallup (2007) reported that 29 percent

Table 2.1 Percentage of Students Enrolled in Grades 3–12 Whose Parents Were Satisfied or Dissatisfied with Various Aspects of Their Children's Schools, by Public- and Private-School Type: 2003 and 2007

	School Type							
	Public, assigned		Public, chosen		Private, religious		Private, non-church	
Parent Satisfaction	2003 (%)	2007 (%)	2003 (%)	2007 (%)	2003 (%)	2007 (%)	2003 (%)	2007 (%)
Very Satisfied with School	54	52	64	62	77	79	72	79
Very Satisfied with Teachers	56	57	65	64	72	76	70	74
Very Satisfied with Academic Standards	55	56	64	66	80	81	77	79
Very Satisfied with Discipline	56	55	65	61	81	83	80	80

Source: U.S. Department of Education, National Center for Education Statistics n.d.

of parents with children in a public-school system would prefer a different education system. A follow-up survey in 2018 found that when answering the question, "In order to improve public education in America, some people think the focus should be on reforming the existing public-school system. Others believe the focus should be on finding an alternative to the existing public-school system. Which approach do you think is preferable—reforming the existing public-school system or finding an alternative to the existing public-school system?" 22 percent of parents wanted to find alternatives.[20] This has been a steady result in every poll since 1997 with a spike to over 30 percent in 2000 and is not just true for the vague concept of the school system but also true when the respondents evaluated their own schools: "Results are similar when it comes to reforming or reconstituting schools in one's own community rather than nationally, with 78 percent preferring reform and 21 percent backing alternatives."[21] A fifth of parents, year in and year out, are so frustrated and disappointed with the public-school system that they would go to an alternative if they could: some try to find ways to adapt, some go to a magnet or a charter school or attend a private school, some stay at their public school, and some start home schools.

Rose and Gallup (2007) also found that 40 percent of parents with children in public school favored vouchers, 61 percent favored partial government funding of private-school tuition (including parochial schools), 39 percent favored total government funding of private-school tuition, and 63 percent favored charter schools.[22] Houston and Toma's (2003) research led them to conclude that

> Households choose not only between different types of public-schools and between public and private schools but, in the current environment, they also can choose to home school. The policy implications of this article are rather strong. The attributes of households and the attributes of the public-school district influence the decision to educate children at home. One of the more interesting results is that income differences within a district significantly influence the home schooling decision. Assuming that higher variance implies more diverse tastes for educational output, this result is not surprising. It suggests that public-schools are less likely to satisfy the body politic the more diverse the population.[23]

In reference to figure 2.4 the data indicates that about half the population is in the shaded region. Rose and Gallup (2007) found less than a third of parents with children in public school favor a new system but significantly larger proportions favor various alternative schools. These people correspond to the non-shaded areas between line A and line B in figure 2.4, people who are dissatisfied but not enough to expend resources on a solution.

Finally, in the regions to the left of line A and to the right of line B in figure 2.4 are the parents willing to expend resources on an alternative education. This dissatisfaction stems from the fact that some parents have a preferred solution far from the solution set—far enough away that the solution set is not a viable alternative from their perspective. This condition puts these parents in conflict with the school organization and creates a condition in which these parents seek a different education solution. Their dissatisfaction level is high enough that they are willing to leave the personally low-cost educational product and seek out a different product or produce their own.

Are We Romantic about Public School?

But there is an important question, if there are significant levels of dissatisfaction with the public schools, then why does the public-school system persist? This is not an original question; it has been well covered in other works (see Rothbard 1971, Chubb and Moe 1990, West 1994 for a few) and consequently an in-depth analysis is not necessary here. However, a brief discussion is in order since it has value to understanding the choice to home school. Some of the answer is in the stability and socialized costs already discussed, but in the 2018 Phi Delta Kappan survey no parent answered that the public-school system was perfect; everyone has something they would change. Some of the discontent may be because the public-school system is one of the most coercive of all government institutions, legally requiring that all children attend and all taxpayers support it. As described earlier, the public-school system is a forced solution, it is stable but not Pareto efficient; consequently, it provides us with too much of some forms of education and not enough of other forms. Some may wonder if the idea of too much education even makes sense, but when the provider of any good or service is insulated from market discipline there will be discoordination that will exemplify itself in persistent shortages and inventories. Some demanders prefer more while others prefer less. Rose and Gallup (2007) demonstrate this problem, in a survey they conducted that asked a series of questions about the public-school curriculum and there was wide disagreement. For example, they found that:

- 48 percent believe public schools teach the right amount of math and science and 48 percent do not;
- 57 percent believe public schools should spend more time on learning about other countries, 40 percent do not;
- 70 percent believe that foreign language education should begin in lower grades, 29 percent believe it should begin in upper grades.[24]

Over half the respondents said the public school does a worse job in preparing students for work and teaching math, a third would change the school schedule, and 30 percent have no confidence that schools are prepared to deal with a shooting. Yet, in the final questions of the survey 70 percent give their child's own school an A or B grade, 43 percent give the schools in their community an A or B while only 19 percent give the national system an A or B.[25]

There are at least two ways to read this. One may be the spotlight affect. Parents know their own child's school best and seem happy with it, although 30 percent did give a C or lower but the news reports on various problems and scandals in others highlight those issues even though most people do not personally experience them; my school is okay, but those schools "out there" seem to be a wreck.

The other interpretation is that the local school has the same issues as the schools "out there" but parents are willing to turn a blind eye or downplay some of these problems and thus have a rosier view of the local school even if it is not completely deserved, that is they are a little romantic about the local school. It is where their child goes and it may be where they also went, they know people who work there and the parents of their child's friends and the school may hold fond memories and associations. The truth is probably somewhere in-between: the national system is probably better than they think but the local school probably is not as good as they think. Regardless of the truth, there is significant disagreement about what public schools should be doing, how much of it they should be doing, and how well they are doing it.

And yet, strong support for the public school system persists. As explained earlier the public-school system provides benefits to many interest groups and one of these benefits is beyond the tangible and political may be psychological or romantic. We see this view on display from a man who believes that public schools provide an inferior education. In his book *The People's Romance*, Professor Dan Klein relates this incident:

> In 1995, the annual meeting of the American Economic Association included a plenary session about domestic policy issues. One of the panelists was the Nobel laureate MIT economist Robert Solow. In the course of his remarks, Solow said that he did not find school choice appealing. During the question-and-answer period, I asked him why he did not find school vouchers appealing. He replied: "It isn't for any economic reason; all the economic reasons favor school vouchers. It is because what made me an American is the United States Army and the public-school system."[26]

While this could obviously open a discussion about what it means to be an American that is beyond my purpose. The point is Professor Solow believed strongly that the economic arguments, which he did not specify in these comments, favor parental choice in education but he rejects the idea because he believes the school system accomplishes other goals he likes. Solow is a superb economist, a Nobel Prize winner with a list of prominent students some of whom have also won the Nobel Prize. A first-rate analytical mind, he has a romantic notion about what the public-school system did for him, which has nothing to do with education and requires him to suspend the economic arguments. He is not alone.

NOTES

1. Bryant, Homeschoolers want you to believe the pandemic has a silver lining – they're wrong, 2020.
2. Bryant 2020.
3. Bryant 2020.
4. Educational Institutions 2019.
5. The Editorial Team 2021.
6. Immerwahr and Johnson 2005.
7. Immerwahr and Johnson 2005.
8. Tullock, Why So Much Stability, 1981, 194.
9. Tullock 1981, 198.
10. Obviously, these different studies have different criteria and look for different things but in the last few years and dating back at least 20 years Finland has been at or near the top of many different rankings. In addition to the OECD referenced see the National Center for Education and the economy (https://ncee.org/what-we-do/center-on-international-education-benchmarking/top-performing-countries/), or The World Top 20 Project (https://worldtop20.org/worldbesteducationsystem).
11. Gamerman, What Makes Finish Kids So Smart 2008.
12. Central Intelligence Agency n.d.
13. Gamerman, What Makes Finish Kids So Smart 2008.
14. Central Intelligence Agency n.d.
15. Gamerman, What Makes Finish Kids So Smart 2008.
16. Tikkanen, Parental school satisfaction in the context of segregation of basic education in urban Finland 2019.
17. Tikkanen 2019.
18. Sable and Hill 2006.
19. National Center for Education Statistics 2010.
20. Phi Delta Kappan 2018.
21. Phi Delta Kappan 2018.
22. Rose and Gallup 2007.
23. Houston and Toma, Homeschooling: An Alternative School Choice, 2003, 934.
24. Rose and Gallup 2007.
25. Rose and Gallup 2007.
26. Klein, The People's Romance: Why People Love Gopvernment (as much as they do) 2005, 5.

Chapter 3

Entrepreneurship Theory and Its Application to the Home School Family

WHAT IS AN ENTREPRENEUR?

Analyzing home school parents as entrepreneurs may strike some as odd; it is probably the case that most home school parents do not think of themselves this way, they are just parents trying to do the best for their children. But the process of how that comes about is an entrepreneurial process and can only be properly understood if analyzed as an entrepreneurial decision.

Entrepreneurs are commonly thought of as profit-seeking business types, but not all businessmen are entrepreneurs and not all entrepreneurs are businessmen. A proper definition of entrepreneur is not about the precise goal they seek but that they act: "[E]ntrepreneur means acting man in regard to the changes occurring in the data of the market."[1] That is not to say that entrepreneurs do not seek profits, of course they do: "entrepreneurs (are) those who are especially eager to profit from adjusting production to the expected changes in conditions, those who have more initiative, more venturesomeness, and a quicker eye than the crowd."[2] I return to this idea of home school profits in a later chapter, the focus here is *how* does an entrepreneur act. What does it mean to be an "acting man" in this context?

Economists are sometimes accused of assuming away important factors in their analysis; an old joke says that an economist solution to being stranded on a desert island is to assume a boat. How much validity is in this stereotype is for others to say but when it comes to entrepreneurs there is some truth in it. Despite the vital role entrepreneurs play in the economy, they have been frequently overlooked by economists. In much economic analysis the role and function and impact of entrepreneurship is given very little consideration and is assumed in the models. However, there are three major figures in economics who spent time thinking and considering the entrepreneur.

Entrepreneur as Creative Destroyer

Joseph Schumpeter (1883–1950) was an Austrian political economist. Born in what is modern-day Czech Republic, Schumpeter was a citizen of the Austrian-Hungarian Empire. His father died when he was four and his mother moved the family to Vienna where he grew up. He earned degrees in economics from the University of Vienna and went on to hold positions in the Austrian government and served as president of a large bank; neither of these went very well and Schumpeter spent most of his life as an academic. He came to the United States in 1932 and took a faculty position at Harvard University. He is considered to be an eclectic thinker not easily slotted into a particular perspective or school of thought. He was a product of what was at the time a robust academic program in political economy in Austria but stood apart from his Austrian contemporaries in many ways in his thinking and economic analysis. However, he was a prolific researcher and teacher and influenced many economists who themselves went on to prominent careers in the field. Schumpeter was the first economist to seriously consider and examine the entrepreneur and entrepreneurship as a vital aspect of the economy.

In his most popular work, *Capitalism, Socialism and Democracy*, published in 1942 but still in print in over a dozen languages, Schumpeter made several bold claims, maybe the boldest is that capitalism is doomed to fail because its benefactors will take its success for granted and fail to defend it from socialism:

> Can capitalism survive? No. I do not think it can. But this opinion of mine, like that of every other economist who has pronounced upon the subject, is in itself completely uninteresting. What counts in any attempt at social prognosis is not the Yes or No that sums up the facts and arguments which lead up to it but those facts and arguments themselves. . . . The thesis I shall endeavor to establish is that the actual and prospective performance of the capitalist system is such as to negative the idea of it breaking down under the weight of economic failure, but that its very success undermines the social institutions which protect it.[3]

Schumpeter did not desire this outcome; he lamented it, but felt it was likely. However, despite this controversial claim, a significant part of this work, and maybe the most important part, is Schumpeter's analysis of the entrepreneur and his introduction of the idea of creative destruction. Schumpeter describes the entrepreneur as a creative crusader taking risks and developing new products and technologies and disrupting the *status quo*:

> The opening up of new markets, foreign or domestic, and the organizational developments from the craft shop and factory to such concerns as U.S. Steel

illustrate the same process of industrial mutation . . . that incessantly revolutionizes the economic structure *from within*, incessantly destroying the old one, incessantly creating a new one. This process of Creative Destruction is the essential fact about capitalism.[4]

To Schumpeter, the market and entrepreneurship is an organic process, natural if allowed to occur without obstruction, and most importantly essential if the capitalist system is to continue to improve human conditions. "We have seen that the function of the entrepreneur is to reform or revolutionize the pattern of production by exploiting an invention or more generally, an untried technological possibility for producing a new source of supply of materials or producing an old one in a new way."[5] Schumpeter goes on to point out why so few people become entrepreneurs:

> To undertake such new things is difficult and constitutes a distinct economic function, first, because they lie outside of the routine tasks that everybody understands and second, because the environment resists in many ways. . . . To act with confidence beyond the range of familiar beacons and to overcome that resistance requires aptitudes that are present in only a small fraction of the population and that define the entrepreneurial type as well as the entrepreneurial function.[6]

To Schumpeter, the entrepreneur is a natural result of a dynamic market system that rearranges the current way of doing things and drives progress and prosperity.

Entrepreneur as Romantic Madman

William Baumol (1922–2017) may be the leading thinker and researcher on entrepreneurship in the neo-classical school. Baumol, like Schumpeter, was a prolific author and respected teacher who simultaneously held positions at Princeton and New York University. The neo-classical tradition in economic analysis has historically not given entrepreneurialism much consideration, but Baumol changed all of that. As a 2006 article in *The Economist* about Baumol's work stated, "Entrepreneurs are the leading men of capitalism, the venturesome protagonists who move the plot forward. But economic theory gives them few if any lines to read."[7] The article goes on to explain the crux of Baumol's work on entrepreneurship:

> Most innovations are merely incremental improvements on something that already exists: a slightly better mousetrap, as Mr Baumol puts it. A rare few represent discontinuous breakthroughs, such as the incandescent lamp, alternating

34   Chapter 3

electric current or the jet engine. All of the above, according to Frederic Scherer, professor emeritus at Harvard, were introduced not by the regimented R&D of established corporations, but by scrappy new firms, twin-born with the invention itself. Mr Baumol ventures that most breakthroughs arise this way—the offspring of independent minds not incumbent companies. He has two explanations for this. First, radical innovation is the only kind lone entrepreneurs can do; and, second, they are the only ones who want to do it.

The first explanation seems paradoxical. Breakthroughs are, by definition, more difficult than routine innovations. Surely, they should be beyond the meagre means of the independent entrepreneur? But as Mr Baumol points out, building the *Kitty Hawk* was much cheaper, and less complicated, than upgrading the Boeing 737 to the 747. Genuinely new ideas are often breathtakingly simple. They grow more elaborate as improvements and modifications are laid on top of them. If you are the first to discover a tree, you get to pick the lowest-hanging fruit.

The second explanation is more intuitive. Revolution is a risky endeavour. Of 1,091 Canadian inventions surveyed in 2003 by Thomas Astebro, of the University of Toronto, only 75 reached the market. Six of these earned returns above 1,400 percent, but 45 lost money. A rational manager will balk at such odds. But the entrepreneur answers to his own dreams and demons. Mr Baumol thinks a "touch of madness" is probably one of the chief qualifications for the job.

Economists have little to say about madness, of course. But they can point out its economic implications. If money isn't everything to the independent inventor, he is likely to be cheap. Indeed, he will be the lowest-cost provider of the kind of risky, painstaking endeavour that lies behind the breakthrough inventions. Big firms could pursue the big ideas, but since they would be employing professionals not amateurs for these quixotic ventures, they would have to pay them in money, not love.

Thanks to Mr Baumol's own painstaking efforts, economists now have a bit more room for entrepreneurs in their theories. But it remains a mystery why anyone would want to be one.[8]

For Baumol the corporate research department is driven by expected returns and actual costs with the full expectation that many innovations will fail so some have to hit big to pay for themselves and the failures. This pushes these large firms toward more expensive but ultimately safer courses of research. It may be more expensive to upgrade the 737 to 747 but Boeing knows there is a market for airline travel, the Wright brothers had no idea if there would be a market for air travel and it may not have even been a consideration. One story says that one brother thought that airplanes would be good for recreation and military scouting and that's it. They were driven by wanting to prove it could be done, not by a vision for global travel. They were engineers and experimenters first and later proved to be competent but not particularly innovative business operators.

Entrepreneur as Alert Observer

Israel Kirzner (b. 1930) is the third of the three economists whose research work focused on entrepreneurs. Kirzner was born in London and raised in England and South Africa but spent most of his career at New York University earning his doctorate there in 1957 and remaining on faculty until his retirement in 2001. In addition to being an economist, Kirzner is also a rabbi and one of the world's leading scholars on the work and teachings of Rabbi Isaac Hunter.

Kirzner begins his discussion by recognizing the truth that "[t]he entrepreneurial role in the market is an elusive one. This is demonstrated in the virtual elimination of this role from most contemporary expositions of price theory," but he goes on to say: "[I]n my view it is possible to pin down the elusive element in a satisfactory way. I further believe that to do so is of the utmost importance to understanding the market process."[9]

Notice that all three of these researchers discuss how the entrepreneur is absent in much of economic theory. It is frustrating to see this important function passed over in the research and literature so much. Kirzner breaks down entrepreneurial action into component parts and begins by criticizing the more simplistic and prevailing idea in economics at the time, outside these three men, an entrepreneur was simply a person who was seeking and found a more efficient way to accomplish a task, what we might think of as entrepreneur as economizer. This is certainly an element of successful entrepreneurship, but to Kirzner it was a far from a complete explanation and certainly fell short of explaining how important entrepreneurship is to the market process:

> I choose to label that element of alertness to possible newly worthwhile goals and to possibly newly available resources—which we have seen is absent from the notion of economizing but very much present in that of human action—the entrepreneurial element in human decision-making. It is this entrepreneurial element that is responsible for our understanding of human action as active, creative and human rather than as passive, automatic and mechanical.[10]

From this, Kirzner proposes the idea of the pure entrepreneur, "a decision-maker whose entire role arises out of his alertness to hitherto unnoticed opportunities."[11] This is a vital observation. Kirzner abstracted the idea of entrepreneurship as the act of discovering an opportunity to coordinate resources more efficiently. But beyond that, Kirzner, unlike many others, sees the intrinsic characteristics, traits, and personality of the entrepreneur as a vital component:

> In order to make a discovery, in this world, it is simply not sufficient to be somehow more prescient than others; it requires that that "abstract" prescience be supported by psychological qualities that encourage one to ignore conventional wisdom, to dismiss the jeers of those deriding what they have seen as the self-deluded visionary, to disrupt what others have come to see as the comfortable familiarity of the old-fashioned ways of doing things, to ruin rudely and even cruelly the confident expectations of those whose somnolence has led them to expect to continue to make their living as they have for years past.[12]

At first glance, Kirzner's entrepreneur and Schumpeter's look like polar opposites. In his initial analysis, Kirzner made some sharp distinctions between his entrepreneur who brings equilibrium and greater coordination and Schumpeter's entrepreneur that brings disequilibrium and creative destruction. In a later work, Kirzner while not fully reconciling with Schumpeter does provide "a clearer understanding of how each of these apparently conflicting views can be seen as plausible and realistic; and how each can usefully advance economic understanding (of respectfully different aspects of a capitalist economy)."[13] The central theme of this reconsideration is expressed in the following four propositions:

1. For understanding the psychological profile typical of the real-world entrepreneur as we know him, Schumpeter's portrayal is valid and accurate.
2. For understanding the "creative destruction" which Schumpeter sees as the central and distinguishing feature of the capitalist system, Schumpeter's portrayal is valid and essential, to the extent that policy objectives include the stimulation of such creative destruction, careful attention will indeed have to be paid to that Schumpeterian psychological profile to which we have referred.
3. For understanding the equilibrative tendency of markets in general, my own view of the entrepreneur as alert to opportunities (created by, or able to be created by, independently initiated changes) is valid and significant.
4. To see the entrepreneurial role of a real-world entrepreneur as essentially that of being "merely" alert to opportunities created (or able to be created) by independently initiated changes is not necessarily inconsistent with a Schumpeterian perspective on the activity of that same entrepreneur (which sees him as aggressively and actively initiating change).[14]

Extending this analysis further we can see more complementary similarities between these two. Schumpeter's creative destroyer is destroying old ways of doing things that may have been efficient and proper at one time (they probably were) but are now outmoded, in need of replacement by better methods, approaches, and techniques. Meanwhile Kirzner's entrepreneur is alert to the fact that fundamental changes in the economic landscape have taken place and is willing to suffer the ridicule of the old guard to prove the point, and possibly profit from it. Meanwhile Baumol argues that this destructive creator landscape changer is much more likely to be a lone operator and not part of an established organization. I am not trying to reconcile these three when they themselves did not do so, but entrepreneurship is multifaceted and these views are more complementary than competing and it should not be a surprise if home schoolers, and all entrepreneurs, display characteristics of all three.

Thinking Creatively about Creators

Besides applying formal entrepreneurship theory to home schoolers, there are some other angles from which to examine home schoolers that provide some further insights.

One comes from the Nobel Prize-winning political economist the late Elinor Ostrom and a variety of co-authors she had, the primary one being her husband, Vincent. Ostrom researched, among other things, the management of common resources and collective-action problems, such as policing and educating children. She pioneered the concept of polycentricity and the idea that emergent solution can address social problems and further argued that it is wrong and even harmful to assume that a monocentric approach, a one-size-fits-all government solution, to these problems is the most effective and efficient.

> Extensive studies of urban service delivery (for overview see McGinnis 1999b) and of common-pool resources (E. Ostrom, Gardner, and Walker 1994; Gibson, McKean, and Ostrom 2000) conducted in association with the Workshop in Political Theory and Policy Analysis at Indiana University, found numerous communities in both urban and rural areas who have self organized to provide and coproduce quality local services, given the constraints that they face. Many policy analysts presume that without major external resources and top down planning by national officials, there can be no provision of public goods and sustainable common-pool resources. This presumption is wrong.
>
> The opposite prescription that local communities will always solve collective-action problems is also wrong. It is a struggle to find effective ways of providing these services, but public entrepreneurs working closely with citizens frequently do find new ways of putting services together using a mixture of local talent and resources (Dietz, Ostrom, and Stern 2003). If governance systems arrange polycentrically, from small to very large, collective-action problems are

solvable on multiple scales. The costs of effective self organization are lower when authority exists to create institutions whose boundaries match the problems faced. External financial resources may increase the options available to a local community. External resources are not the essential ingredient for building an effective public sector to provide local public goods and protect smaller scale common-pool resources. The results achieved have been grossly disappointing, for example solving local problems with the allocation of massive amounts of donor funds. (Gibson et al. 2005)

The presumption that locals cannot take care of public sector problems has led to legislation throughout the world that places responsibility for local public services on units of government that are very large, frequently lack the resources to carry out and are overwhelmed with their assignment. Contemporary assignments of regional, national, or international governments with exclusive responsibility for providing local public goods and common-pool resources removes authority from local officials and citizens to solve local problems that differ from one location to the next.[15]

While she was not thinking of home schooling, Ostrom is arguing that local entrepreneurs are often, although not always, able to provide a public service much better than a top-down planned and government organized approach. The presumption that local units and private actors, the polycentric approach, are incapable has led to some ineffective and inefficient policies, especially in situations where the problems and the solution will differ in different places. This describes home schooling rather well, every child is different and the private actor, the parent as education entrepreneur, can and does develop a solution that applies exclusively to their children. And the next unit (home school) develops a different approach. In Ostrom's model it is not surprising that a polycentric approach outperforms the monocentric approach, to put it in terms for this analysis, that many home schools are as successful (or more successful, this discussion is in a later chapter) than the public school.

Another angle to consider is offered by author, speaker, editor, and economist Jeffrey Tucker. In his lecture, *Capitalism Is Love*, Tucker describes the way the market system engenders and encourages four different kinds of loves. Using C. S. Lewis' book *The Four Loves* as a model, Tucker lays out the four different loves found in the Greek language and discussed in the Bible. Tucker describes entrepreneurialism as being akin to *eros*, romantic love. In a gentle and humorous way he calls it a form of insanity but he connects the joy that comes from the idea of life with the one you love with the joy an entrepreneur feels in imagining how life could be different if he is able to make his idea a reality.[16]

It is crazy to think that a family could outperform the long-established professional education system. Choosing to try is not driven by profits, although

I discuss the profit concept applied to home schooling in a later chapter, it is first driven by love, parental love for a child, which is closer to *agape* than *eros* but on the same spectrum. As Tucker says, "it (the act of entrepreneurship) is not the desperate love of money, if that were it, entrepreneurship, for the most part, would be a stupid thing to do because almost everybody fails . . . it's not money, it's the love of an idea."[17] And I might add the love for the people you want to serve. In a traditional business this love would not be *eros* but *storge* or possibly *philos* but with a home school this touch of madness exhibits itself as all four loves.

ENTREPRENEURIAL ANALYSIS APPLIED TO HOME SCHOOLING

The individual home school family, especially the early adopters and the successful ones at any stage, primarily fit the Kirznerian entrepreneurship model. They are dissatisfied, alert to changes in the cost of education and that created opportunities to produce a better outcome. But there is also some Baumol aspect to what they do as they have pioneered new technologies and new models of doing things like unschooling and changing the school day, week, and year and experimenting with different approaches. And, as a group, they put Schumpeterian style pressures on an antiquated system forcing either change or, in some cases resistance, from the old institutions. This is all being driven by a parental love and is successful because of its polycentric nature which allows adaptability and flexibility the monocentric institution cannot match.

Home Schoolers as Alert Observers

The individual home school family often has one of Kirzner's pure entrepreneurs; someone in the family, sometimes a child, who sees there are better options for education than the public school. This alertness does not always manifest itself in the realization of what the better option might be, but it frequently starts with the child complaining, not doing well, being frustrated, and generally having a bad school experience. This may not be what we might think of as alertness along the lines of business entrepreneurs or inventors but it is the first signal, the first bit of information that something in the current approach is not working as this story of a reluctant parent and entrepreneurial child demonstrates:

> Four years ago, Alicia Knight would have been the last person you could ever imagine home schooling her kids.

> She was a very active parent in the Stafford County, Va., public-schools, where her son Roger was a fifth grader.... Whenever her son struggled with his homework, which was often, she said: "You've just got to get this school work done because, with God as my witness, I'm NOT home schooling you!"
>
> Alicia Knight, the die-hard anti-home schooler, changed her mind gradually. The first person to work on her was her own son, who heard her say she was never going to home school him and took that to mean that homeschooling was a viable alternative to the torture he was suffering at school and with homework. She resisted. She tried testing, child study meetings, educational consultants and high-priced tutors. But "by the time my son was in the fifth grade and thoroughly miserable, I was willing to do anything—even if it meant having to bite my tongue and join up with the wing-nuts who I thought dominated the home schooling scene," she said ... on the first day of her uncertain new life as a home schooling mom, her son walked into her home office with a stack of books under his arm. "Hey Mom," he said. "These are all the books that I've been wanting to read but never had a chance. Can I read them now?" He read for 11 hours that day and 10 hours the next. She decided this might not be so bad after all.[18]

In this story, Alicia, the mother, at first was the one launching the jeers and derision. Her wing-nut comment may have political implications but also evokes Baumol's touch of madness characterization. But her son Roger was the pure entrepreneur, first by being miserable and then in conversations with his mom until she eventually agreed. I would also point out this story contradicts much of the standard criticisms of home schooling, this was not about parents dragging kids out of school, it was not motivated by religion or alternate lifestyle choices, it was about a parents' love for a struggling child and what was best for ten-year-old Roger who was miserable and just wanted to read.

Of course, not every home school family goes through this sort of experience; some begin home schooling on day one and the parents are the ones alert to an alternative that will meet their goals and fit their family better. But they too can often be the target of ridicule, if not by friends and family, which does happen, then certainly by elements of society and the education establishment especially in the early years. But the point is *someone* is alert to a better way. The child as pure entrepreneur is seeking relief from his or her misery, the parent as a pure entrepreneur is a bit more sophisticated and meets Kirzner's criteria in a different way: "For me the function of the entrepreneur consists not of shifting the curves of cost or of revenues which face him, but of noticing that they have in fact shifted."[19] For the home school parent it is especially important that those cost curves have changed. The home school parent looked at the education terrain and saw a system that has not changed in any real way in over 100 years, despite the fact that education is much less costly to obtain than it once was. The cost curves have shifted and the traditional public school is locked into an old model which is not only no longer cost efficient but the schools have not noticed the changes or, if they have, they will not or cannot respond. This is changing a bit with the onset of school shutdowns due to the Covid virus but not that much as it appears that the old ways are largely set to return but there are some signs of innovation such as the discussion of micro-schools.

Home school parents have ignored the conventional wisdom that a professionalized public school is best; dismissed the jeers from the press, politicians, and experts; and confidently (in most cases) met the challenge posed by the monolithic institutions that comprise the public education system and, by many measures and producing a better student and creating Schumpeterian pressures that have been resisted by the political insulated, so far.

Home Schooling as Creative Destruction

While no home school parent has the expressed desire to reform the public-school system, the collective success of their enterprises has exerted some significant pressures on the old system. If the American education system was a free market, by that I mean parents have complete choice of where to send their children and schools had to attract students by offering better value, the public system probably would have changed and responded many times over the years but even if it had not, the success of a relatively small subset of education establishments called home schools might have forced a response. But the public system is politically insulated from such pressures and its interest groups responded to these pressures by appealing to its political patrons, seeking to enforce all sorts of rules and regulations on home schools ranging from applying truancy laws to pushing to require parents to be licensed teachers or requiring home schools to use board of education approved curriculum. The list of political responses is long and varied. However, home schoolers have not been without the will and ability to fight a political fight and have forced changes to public policy, if not public schools, largely through the courts which are not party to the education solution set. While the process has been frustrated by interest group politics, the Schumpeterian pressures are present. That such a small group, never more than 3 percent of the national student body evoked and continues to evoke such strong responses from so many who are tied to the old ways of doing things shows a strong fear that creative destruction is not far off. Covid has made those fears more present.

Other less politically insulated more market-oriented institutions have responded in a much more positive way. Various public and private institutions have changed to accommodate the needs of home school families, museums, art galleries, athletic leagues (even in some cases and some places the public schools—a little) have all changed. These places host home school days, have programs for home school students, and have even changed their hours of operation. This may not be creative destruction in the purest Schumpeterian sense but it is creative reforms *and* has brought better coordination between one group of students and these institutions.

ARE HOME SCHOOL FAMILIES ENTREPRENEURS?

It is one thing to discuss the theoretical aspects of entrepreneurs and see how those apply to home school families but real-world entrepreneurs have been studied and have been found to possess certain kinds of characteristics and behaviors and ways of thinking. The research reveals that those willing to take the risk to start a new business share several common characteristics, even across international borders. If home school parents are truly entrepreneurial, then it is logical that they should share many of these same characteristics that are found in other types of entrepreneurs. What follows is a character study of home school parents and business entrepreneurs.

There is no way to identify entrepreneurs in the von Misean sense, and for research purposes the best proxy we can use is the self-employed. It is an admittedly limited proxy, not all entrepreneurs are self-employed and not all self-employed are entrepreneurs, but it is a useful proxy and maybe the best available. According to the Bureau of Census's 2000 Consumer Population Survey (CPS), America's self-employed share a variety of common characteristics. The self-employed marry at higher rates than the rest of the population and are overwhelmingly white and are better educated than the general population.[20] Some characteristics, which I omitted, such as the majority are middle income, are not unique or informative. However, the education level, marriage rates, and ethnic breakdown are different from the general population and provide a set of objective measures to which home school parents can be compared, but these are not the only characteristics to consider. Southern Methodist University's Cox School of Business conducted a research project on the characteristics of successful entrepreneurs. They defined success as a business with gross revenues over $1 million or five years in existence. The researchers identified twelve characteristics: good health, need to control, self-confidence, sense of urgency, comprehensive awareness, realistic outlook, conceptual ability, low need for status, objective approach, emotional stability, attraction to challenges, and number oriented.[21]

I did not attempt to analyze every factor the Cox School identified; large-scale data for such a comparison does not exist, but I did analyze what could be and found considerable congruence between business entrepreneurs and home school families. As Lines (2000) found, home school families tend to be "more religious, more conservative, somewhat more affluent, and headed by parents with somewhat more education."[22] Much of the same could be said for business entrepreneurs as well.

Marital Status

As the CPS shows, almost 74 percent of business entrepreneurs are married. Every study of home school family characteristics finds that the overwhelming majority of home school parents are married. Ray (1997) found that 98 percent of home school families were headed by married couples.[23] Rudner (1999) found that 97 percent of home school parents were married.[24] Bauman (2002) found that 88 percent of home school families were headed by a married couple,[25] and the Department of Education's National Center for Education Statistics (2005) found a lower but still high marriage rate of 81 percent.[26] And, the National Household Education Survey (2012) found 79 percent of home school families are headed by a married couple.[27] Meanwhile marriage rates among the general population have always been lower. In 1980, 61 percent of American households were headed by a married couple and by 2017 that number was just below 50 percent with only 19 percent of American households headed by a married couple who also had children in the home.[28]

Both the self-employed and home school families have a marriage rate that exceeds the general population but they are not immune from general trends as the percentage of home school families that are headed by married couples has fallen over time just as in the general population. But the point here is that there seems to be correlation between entrepreneurship and marriage, the research is thin on this relationship but all point to a linkage between self-employment and marriage: "the relationship between marital status and self-employment has been only very crudely analyzed in the empirical literature, although evidence from the cross-sectional data repeatedly shows that the married are overrepresented among the self-employed"[29] and educational entrepreneurs reflect that. It is assumed that home school families are predominantly married households because one parent needs to be the teacher. As I show in the coming chapters the idea of a parent as teacher has some truth in it but it is a significant over simplification of how successful home schooling works. It is possible some of the reason home schooling is predominantly comprised of married households are the same reasons the self-employed are. This relationship is definitely a ripe area for further exploration.

Racial Demographics

The CPS found that small business owners were 90 percent white. This is a gap that has persisted over time and consistently shows up in the research: "There are also some sharp differences by race and ethnicity. White workers were more than twice as likely as black workers to be self-employed in 2014, 11 percent versus 5 percent. Meanwhile, the rate of self-employment was 10 percent among Asian workers and 8 percent among Hispanic workers. These gaps have persisted for a long period of time."[30] However, Reynolds et al. (2002) found that both blacks and Hispanics were engaging in new entrepreneurial activity at a higher rate than before and the next entrepreneur is more likely to be a minority than was likely a few years ago. Home school trends seem to be moving in the same direction and maybe even at a faster pace. Home school families have been overwhelmingly white but the trend is toward racial diversity. Ray (1997) found that 96 percent of home school families were white[31] while Bauman (2002) found that 92 percent were white.[32] The most recent data shows that 59 percent of home school students are white, 26 percent Hispanic, and 8 percent black compared to the general student population which is 50 percent white, 24 percent Hispanic, and 14 percent black.[33] This mirrors the trends in business ownership as well: "Minority-owned firms accounted for 28.8 percent of all U.S. firms in 2012."[34]

When it comes to racial demographics home school families once looked like the self-employed but seem to have diversified more over the last fifteen years, but racial diversification is a trend in both groups.

Education Level

A significant number of business entrepreneurs have attended college, which makes them more educated than the general population. In their study of 830 nascent American entrepreneurs entitled *The Entrepreneur Next Door* Reynolds et al. (2002) found that education had a positive impact on the likelihood of starting a business. "Individuals who finish high school and complete some additional education or training are more likely to be involved in the entrepreneurial process."[35] But this does not tell the full story, over 40 percent of male and over 25 percent of female entrepreneurs had completed college or graduate school. Reynolds and his colleagues are supported in their findings by several other studies. The 2002 U.S. census found that "at the time they started or acquired ownership of their business; twenty-three percent had a bachelor's degree; and seventeen percent had a graduate degree."[36]

Education statistics for home school parents look remarkably similar to business entrepreneurs as shown in table 3.1.

Table 3.1 Parental Education Levels and Home Schooling

Study	Date	Finding
National Center for Education Statistics	1999	49 percent of home school parents had at least a four-year degree.[37]
Scholastic Achievement and Demographic Characteristics of Home School Students	1999	66.2 percent of fathers and 56.7percent of mothers have at least four-year college degrees.[38]
Education Policy Analysis (Belfield)	2004	"Higher maternal education is strong influence on homeschooling."[39]
National Household Education Surveys Program	2016	15 percent have at least a parent with a graduate degree. 30 percent have at least a parent with a four-year degree.[40]

Religion

One characteristic that was not included in the studies cited earlier is religious beliefs: however, several attitudinal or worldview characteristics were mentioned and these are often tied to religious belief. Plus, given the public perception that many home school families are religiously motivated it is important to discuss religion. Since Max Weber (1905) there has been interest and research into his theses that Protestant Christianity has or had a causal effect on the development of a capitalist economic system. While that debate is for another work, the idea that religion has an impact on economic systems should not be dismissed, and its specific impact on entrepreneurialism may be important.

Is it possible that religious views are incidental or at least secondary to the decision to home school? Ray (2004) found that 77 percent of home school families cite religious reasons for home schooling[41] and it is logical that devoutly religious people have a greater dissatisfaction with the median education the public-school system offers. But that does not mean that all who have religious-based dissatisfaction automatically become education entrepreneurs. There are many schools available that have religious focus; over 5,000 Catholic Schools and over 15,000 other religiously affiliated schools ranging from conservative Christian to non-Christian. Most of these tend to be small with a significant amount of parental involvement and control. If religion was the main issue there are choices beside home schooling. Maybe those of certain religious beliefs are just more likely to be entrepreneurial in general.

To examine this possibility, I leave the United States and look at a study on entrepreneurship in Brazil, a predominantly Catholic country. Djankov, Qian, Roland, and Zhuravskaya (2008) conducted research on the characteristics of Brazilian entrepreneurs. They found many things that correlate with the aforementioned findings such as entrepreneurs are more likely to be married and better educated.[42] They also found in a country that is only 9 percent Protestant, that 15 percent of entrepreneurs were Protestant. In a statistical test of significance Djankov et al. found Protestantism to be a significant predictor of entrepreneurialism at the 5 percent level.[43]

I will not revisit Max Weber and his thesis about Protestantism and Capitalism but there may be some interesting applications to that conversation from these findings, the authors themselves cite him but my application is that Protestants are a minority in Brazil. To the extent that people take their religion seriously they see things fundamentally differently than the prevailing culture. Those outside Christianity looking in may not see it but there are differences and a Protestant in Catholic Brazil may be more likely to see opportunities that others do not just as it is more likely that immigrants are self-employed and business owners in the United States than the native born. These folks who have different worldviews and cultural backgrounds may be more likely to have Kirznerian alertness. No one would say that Protestant Christianity is a minority view in the United States but in some circles, at least some versions of it, as discussed in chapter 1, are a fading view and it may be that those with non-mainstream views, regardless of what those views are, Protestants in Catholic Brazil, immigrants in the United States, or orthodox Christians or hippies in modern-day public schools have some sort of naturally heightened alertness that makes them more likely to engage in entrepreneurial activities.

Subjective Characteristics

In addition to the objective measures, research has also uncovered a series of subjective characteristics about the entrepreneur. While many of these subjective measures can be construed and used to support many different hypotheses and I want to be careful about data hallucinations, I believe the evidence supports the idea that home school parents truly fit the entrepreneurial profile.

According to the Cox School report, entrepreneurs have a need to control and direct the environment in which they operate. This would appear to be self-evident for educational entrepreneurs; they abandon the organized public and private school to design their children's curriculum and have a better ability to monitor their children's education, friends, and activities. Ray (2004) found that 32 percent of home school parents want to guide their children's social interactions, 74 percent want to teach their belief system, 49 percent want to individualize the curriculum they teach and 47 percent want to control the learning environment.[44] All of these are about directing their children's environment.

The Cox School report also mentions three factors they refer to as comprehensive awareness, realistic outlook, and conceptual ability. In a nutshell, this is the ability to understand the total situation clearly and to see an idea through any intervening disruptions and problems. This maps very nicely to Kirzner's alertness characteristic and the description of an entrepreneur needed to persevere through criticisms and obstacles. The entrepreneur sees something others do not. He can envisage the problems he may face and the means to solve them to reach the desired goal. He is able to form alternate plans and see them through in spite of any obstacles and disruptions. This is an accurate description of an educational entrepreneur's decision and the fall out that often comes from it. For instance, besides the well-documented political and media criticisms and even insults at times, many education entrepreneurs have had to overcome domestic resistance. Ray (1997) found that 60 percent of paternal grandparents and about half of maternal grandparents initially opposed the family's decision to home school.[45] It takes confidence to stand up to one's mother and father in this matter and even more so to stand up to one's in-laws.

The last subjective trait I will discuss from the Cox School Report is a low need for status. Those choosing to home school have been and occasionally still are regularly ridiculed and criticized in a myriad of ways. This refers to the social capital discussion from chapter 2, if the home school family is part of a subculture then the low status corresponds to the social network connectivity. It is similar to the position immigrants and religious minorities find themselves in.

The Evidence Is in . . . Sort Of

This examination of entrepreneurial characteristics and traits suggests that home school parents have many of the same characteristics as business entrepreneurs, but it could be argued that many people have these characteristics. I do not claim there is anything conclusive in this analysis alone, but there is striking consistency with the overall picture that home school parents are true entrepreneurs.

NOTES

1. Mises 1949:1998, 255.
2. Mises 1949:1998, 255.
3. Schumpeter, Capitalism, Socialsm and Democracy,1942 (1976), 61.
4. Schumpeter 1942 (1976), 83.
5. Schumpeter 1942 (1976), 132.

6. Schumpeter 1942 (1976), 132.
7. Searching for the invisible man 2006.
8. Searching for the invisible man 2006.
9. Kirzner 1973, 30.
10. Kirzner 1973, 35.
11. Kirzner 1973, 35.
12. Kirzner 1973, 39.
13. Kirzner, Creativity and/or Alertness: A Reconsideration of the Schumpeterian Entrepreneur 1999, 1.
14. Kirzner, Creativity and/or Alertness: A Reconsideration of the Schumpeterian Entrepreneur 1999, 1.
15. Ostrom, Polycentric systems as one approach for solving collective-action problems 2008, 2–3.
16. Tucker 2015.
17. Tucker 2015.
18. Matthews 2004.
19. Kirzner, Competition and Entrepreneurship 1973, 81.
20. Maraville 2000.
21. Glick-Smith 2008.
22. Lines 2000.
23. Ray, Strengths of Their Own 1997, 29.
24. Rudner, Scholastic Achievement and Demographic Characteristicsof Home School Students in 1999, 1999, 7.
25. Bauman 2002, 22.
26. U.S. Department of Education 2005.
27. Coalition for Responsible Home Education 2020.
28. Vanorman and Jacobsen 2020.
29. Ozcan Only the Lonely? The Influence of the spouse on the transtiontion to self-employment, 2011, 466.
30. Pew Research Center: Social and Demopgraphic Trends 2015.
31. Ray, Strengths of Their Own 1997.
32. Bauman 2002, 22.
33. Coalition for Responsible Home Education 2020.
34. U.S. Census Bureau 2015.
35. Reynolds et al., The Entrepreneur Next Door, 2002, 17.
36. U.S. Census Bureua 2002.
37. National Center for Education Statistics 2010.
38. Rudner 1999.
39. Belfield 2004.
40. Coalition for Responsible Home Education 2020.
41. Ray, Home Educated and Now Adults 2004, 27.
42. Djankov et al. 2007.
43. Djankov et al. 2007.
44. Ray 2004, 27.
45. Ray, Strengths of Their Own 1997, 46.

Chapter 4

Entrepreneurship in Education
What Home Schools Do

IT IS NOT THE STEREOTYPE

Home schoolers face a daunting task, to produce as good or a better education as public schools with a fraction of the resources. If entrepreneurial creativity was ever necessary, it would be in this situation. This chapter examines this creative problem solving. It explores the methods and approaches successful home school families use and shows that successful home schooling is not just replicating school at home but is truly building a private enterprise that is different and unique. For home schools to be successful they must fully exploit their advantages and compensate for their weaknesses. To do this, they employ a variety of techniques and methods most of which fit into two broad categories: network building and customization.

Network Building

Successful home school families build extensive educational networks. Unlike the stereotype that still persists, successful home schooling is not mom and the children sitting around a kitchen table or in front of a makeshift white board with the kids going through books together. That does happen and maybe in the earliest years a home school was essentially a mom, children, and a kitchen table, but even then, that was less true than some might believe as this excerpt from a 1978 *Time* article shows.

> Educational Theorist John Holt, author of *Why Children Fail*, used to tour the lecture circuit trying to persuade elementary and secondary schools to ease rigid rules and cut red tape. No longer. Despairing of reform within the nation's

educational establishment, Holt has now decided to proselytize among parents, urging them to keep their children out of school and teach them at home.

More and more parents are becoming disenchanted with rigid programs, school strikes and the reluctance of teachers to accept responsibility for students' failures to learn.

Parents of some 1,200 children in California's San Fernando Valley have set up small home classes in protest against a local busing order; most say they object not to integration but to their kids' spending one to three hours a day on school buses. Then too there are parents who teach their own youngsters because they have decided to pull up stakes and spend a few months or even years touring the U.S. in mobile homes.

One family with two boys who have never been enrolled in school lives on a small farm in Sheffield, Mass. Both parents read to their sons, aged eleven and nine, take them on hikes and involve them in farm chores; their mother, a college graduate, also takes them to special art, poetry and music classes in town. "They decide when and whether they'll learn something," says she. "We help them when they ask, but I'm more interested in how happy people are than if they can stand on their heads."[1]

This article provides a brief glimpse into what was a new phenomenon in 1978 but does a very good job in a few paragraphs of providing an accurate image of home school; an enterprise that is unique to each family but all with much more going on than can be done around a kitchen table. Sure, there is much that happens at home, books must be read, and assignments completed and yes, it is primarily moms, leading the teaching. So, the stereotype is not without validity, but it is very incomplete and focuses on the edges while missing the key advantage of home schooling; being able to get out of the house and build unique education networks. Many parents desire their children to be unique in some way, not to be at the median. No parent dreams that their child grows up to be average. The education theorist mentioned in the article, John Holt, gave voice to this parental dream later in the article: "The best preparation for bad experience is good—and anyway I don't want to prepare people to get along. I want them to resist, to change society for the better."[2]

If the primary reason to home school was to have mom as a teacher instead of the one hired by the school system, then that would probably not be much of an advantage, I actually suspect it would be a significant disadvantage. While parental control is an advantage, it is not because parents are superior instructors. In that contest parents are woefully disadvantaged, school teachers are trained professionals whose main occupation is to instruct children, parents are almost never trained educational professionals. The primary value-added contribution of the parents in home schooling is building an education network for the child based on the parents' superior knowledge of the child, not the material or teaching methods.

A network is a collection of people and resources with which the home school family has formed relationships for education purposes. However, from a research standpoint identifying and testing for network connectivity is not easy. One cannot ask a single question or even a series of questions and get to the matter efficiently. Identifying and understanding these networks means looking at home schools differently than most researchers have.

For example, many studies find that home school children are actively involved in community activities. In his review of the research up to that point, noted psychologist and home school researcher Richard Medlin reported that:

> [R]esearch on home schooling appeared in the mid-1980s, and an early case study first hinted that home schooled children were perhaps not so isolated as most people seemed to think. Schemmer (1985) observed four home schooling families and noted (with a trace of surprise?) that the children participated in activities outside the home and were "able to communicate with the researcher" (Ray & Wartes, 1991, p. 56). Since then, several surveys—some of them quite large—asked home schooling parents to report their children's activities. These surveys showed that almost all home school children regularly took part in extracurricular activities (Delahooke, 1986; Gustafson, 1988; Montgomery, 1989; Rakestraw, 1988; Ray, 1990, 1997; Rudner, 1999; Tillman, 1995; Wartes, 1988, 1990). In fact, Delahooke *found that home schooled children actually participated in more activities than did children attending a conventional school. . . . After examining the nature of home schooled children's activities,* Montgomery (1989) *concluded that home schooling parents were purposefully giving their children opportunities to develop leadership abilities.*[3] (emphasis added)

But almost all of these studies and reports use this information to address the question about how well home school students are socialized and miss the fact that these findings point to a larger issue that is a key to understanding home school success. In many reports, networks are implicitly present but not directly addressed or examined. Just one short story appearing in April 27, 2003, issue of *The Washington Times* demonstrates this fact very well. The article mentions a science club, a swim team, study groups for Advanced Placement exams, cultural group, dance classes, theater group, and the Home school Sports Network (with twenty-six basketball teams). All of these were exclusively for home school children. Brian Ray, who was interviewed for the article, "estimates that the average home schooler is involved in five outside activities."[4] Nowhere in the article did it discuss the educational value of these networks or how parents went about building them.

Each home school is its own educational enterprise and has a unique network with connections and relationships appropriate to its goals and students. While these networks are visible, they are not easily understood. Physically counting outside activities or trips to the library is fine and useful up to a point, but these activities are not unique to home school students, the difference is the nature and quality of these visits. The educational difference for home schoolers is not created by piling activity upon activity, but by assembling a unique educational network tailored for each child. Much like piling up a bunch of fabric, even high-quality fabric is not the same as making a wearable outfit. It is about the skill and knowledge to make a quality tailored suit or a quality tailored network.

Network building is exactly what Kirzner says an entrepreneur does. Parents, like everyone, have limited subject knowledge and lack resources for subjects like science, music, and the arts or the notoriously panic inducing advanced math courses. Home school parents cannot possibly acquire the knowledge or afford the equipment and they know this. Kirzner describes what an entrepreneur does when faced with a resource deficiency:

> I speak of the essentially entrepreneurial element in human action in terms of *alertness* to information, rather than of its possession. The entrepreneur is the person who hires the services of factors of production. Among these factors may be persons of superior knowledge. . . . It is the [entrepreneurs] who "know" whom to hire, who "knows" where to find those with market information.[5]

And, this is exactly what parents do: they hire or acquire the resources they need to provide the education they desire for their child. In a 2012 survey of 20,000 home school families by the Home Educating Family Association (HEDUA) the respondents reveal the network building tendencies even though the question was not specifically asked, confirming previous studies that their students participate in sports, music, drama, speech, debate, and several other activities.[6] This reflects Kirzner's idea of an entrepreneur going out and hiring the superior knowledge needed. This is network building.

Networks with More Permanence

But, you may be asking, is not network building just another way to say hire someone? How is this really different from what other families do? A fair thought, but network building is more than just hiring someone, it is more expansive and can take different forms far beyond what a non-home school family does. If one views network building as little more than acquiring assistance on a subject then its purpose and form is not different, but this is just the most basic version and it is not unique to home schools. Getting extra help from a teacher or hiring a tutor or joining a sports team is not uncommon in any school setting. It addresses a problem unique to home school parents in its magnitude but not in its basic form. But this is just one part of a larger picture. When you have a plumbing problem beyond your skill set you hire a plumber, is that building a network? Well, in one sense yes but in another no, it is just a transaction. But if you own a construction firm and need plumbing services on a regular basis then it becomes a network and that is more like home schooling, a long-term building project.

Home school families build many interlocking and overlapping networks. Some are temporary to achieve a specific goal like hiring an expert to fill an academic gap but many have more permanence. Probably the most basic long-term networks home school families build are the internet groups and chat rooms. Eighty-three percent of respondents in the HEDUA survey report using social media for help in home schooling, 62 percent report regularly reading at least one home school blog, and 56 percent report being a member of at least one home school Facebook group.[7] These are trade networks where parents can exchange ideas and thoughts, compare curricula, and discuss problems. Educational entrepreneurs know they are disadvantaged; while they have superior knowledge of their child, what we might call local knowledge, they have limited market knowledge. Their education plans are often constrained by their lack of knowledge of where to find the best resources. As Hayek observed:

> The peculiar character of the problem of a rational economic order is determined precisely by the fact that the knowledge of the circumstances of which we must make use never exists in concentrated or integrated form but solely as the dispersed bits of incomplete and frequently contradictory knowledge which all the separate individuals possess. The economic problem of society is thus not merely a problem of how to allocate "given" resources—if "given" is taken to mean given to a single mind which deliberately solves the problem set by these "data." It is rather a problem of how to secure the best use of resources known to any of the members of society, for ends whose relative importance only these individuals know. Or, to put it briefly, it is a problem of the utilization of knowledge which is not given to anyone in its totality.[8]

This incomplete knowledge is, at least partially, addressed through internet resources that serve as places to combine diverse and dispersed bits of market knowledge into a source of more complete and more usable market knowledge. The internet has been an essential tool in the expeditious spread of home schooling. There are literally hundreds of internet-based chat groups, blogs, and so forth designed to share information among home school families of all types. A quick search reveals groups for home schoolers who are

Christian, Jewish, Muslim, atheist, Wiccans, college bound, and those looking to go into trades, and on and on, it is not unusual for a family to participate in several. Five percent of families in the HEDUA survey report reading at least ten home school blogs on a regular basis.[9]

These internet groups are a virtual market, where one piece of information is exchanged for another and develop into an emergent public good. After all no less an authority than Adam Smith argues that language and communication are foundational to economic exchange:

> Adam Smith set down a theory of language functions and linguistic communication which is relevant to economic behavior. Smith points out in WN (The Wealth of Nations) that the division of labour and cooperation are a natural consequence of the persuasive use of language. . . . Interestingly, Smith assumes this persuasive use of language to be the stimulating factor behind exchange, or trade. . . . The claim that language and the division of labour are inherently linked to the concept of persuasion originates from Smith and implies, as a necessary consequence, the idea that language is a method of communication employed for social cooperation.[10]

These internet groups which are exchanges in language are the beginning but by no means the end of the development of various sort of markets and exchange among home schoolers.

In his 1937 paper, Coase explained out that transactions costs often result in suboptimal allocations in the provision of goods. High transactions costs make hiring resources and the firm structure more efficient than acquiring them in the marketplace as needed. Lower transactions costs allow for more efficient allocation of goods, services, and information and make the firm structure suboptimal.[11] Knowledge used to be expensive. The lecture format still widely in use today in part comes from a time when books were very expensive and the professor was the only person to own one and he would read to the class from his copy. While any college student knows books are still expensive, much has changed and while the transactions costs to participate in an internet group are not zero, they are extremely low. In a different environment, say a world without the internet of thirty years ago, with high transactions costs a parallel substitute for the internet groups would most likely not have emerged, or been much less immediate and useful like a monthly newsletter, and the information provided on them would remain largely dispersed. In such a world the school model makes much more sense from an efficiency point of view and is at least a partial explanation why it was the model of choice for so long. Hiring expertise and establishing a central repository where knowledge and education could be obtained and exchanged, called a school, makes sense when knowledge was relatively expensive. But it is significantly less now.

Researchers estimate that it took humans 1,500 years to double the amount of knowledge we collectively had in 1 AD, it took 250 years to double that, now it is estimated that we double our knowledge every 11–12 hours.[12] Even if these exact numbers are grossly exaggerated the trend is accurate and the quantity of knowledge is increasing rapidly, which makes it very difficult for a central repository to keep current. A standard repository of knowledge for over 200 years has been *The Encyclopedia Britannica.* These were expensive and often passed down as family heirlooms and frequently the first place students would look on any subject. In 2012 the publisher stopped publishing those beautiful encyclopedia sets because it was too expensive and they could not keep up with the changes. There is an online version one can subscribe to but instead of referring to the expertly produced Britannica, it seems the first choice reference source appears to be the emergent public good Wikipedia with its "6,246,119 articles and . . . average [of] 598 new articles per day."[13]

With the low costs of the internet, an overwhelming amount of information can be easily obtained and shared so that each entrepreneur's bit of market knowledge can become public knowledge and can keep better pace with the growing body of knowledge in almost real time. Home schools do not have to wait for the next edition of the text; they have much more flexibility to adjust in real time. Kirzner shows that one aspect of successful entrepreneurship is recognizing that costs have changed and finding ways to exploit these changes before others.[14] The technological changes that resulted in lowering the cost of obtaining and disseminating information have been a key component in home schooling's growth beyond the original subcultures. It has allowed the more alert entrepreneurs to exploit an opportunity and to reduce dissatisfaction, or as Kirzner might say bring better coordination to the market, for them as individuals as well as to the system as a whole.

From Virtual Markets to Physical Markets

In some ways, the physical extension of the internet group is the home school co-op. However, unlike the internet group which is a public good, the co-op is a private good. A co-op is a collection of home school parents who come together one or more times a week to educate their children. It is one way some parents may address resource deficiencies they face but co-ops come with a large variety of goals and purposes ranging from core courses to enrichment classes to specialized instruction. They may look school-like to the outside observer and a few have developed into schools; but the co-op has its foundation on the home school model not on the school organization bureaucratic model. The co-op is a market place not a government bureaucracy. Much as a shopping center and a government office may look architecturally similar but are very different in their purpose, operation, and functionality, so too is the co-op and the school. A co-op is an educational open-air street market where each parent is a vendor offering some sort of educational product or support service from which the other parents may choose. Some parents may teach, some may watch smaller children, and some may do clean-up or administrative work or other tasks. Some co-ops hire tutors or outside experts and some exclusively use parents as teachers but in essence, a co-op is a market place where educational entrepreneurs exchange their expertise.

Co-ops are prevalent and a cottage industry has emerged for helping establish and serve the needs of co-ops. There are books on how to start and run co-ops and consultants who help co-ops with management and administrative issues. The more formalized co-ops are less prevalent, most are not so large or formal, they develop and operate for a few years and then may cease or change as new parents join and old ones leave, they are very dynamic market places. Given the emergent nature of the co-op it is very difficult to know exactly how many there are and how many home school families participate but in the HEDUA survey 45 percent of parents report belonging to at least one co-op.[15] In perusing the internet, one can find co-ops focused on music, cross-cultural studies, vocational skills, as well as those that bill themselves as providing supplemental education in a wide variety of areas. Co-ops are varied and flexible in ways that are impossible for schools to duplicate.

All Visits Are Not Created Equal: Quality Is the Key

This emphasis on network building may seem a little misplaced or something of a false argument, after all public-school families can build networks and they do. But quality is the difference. Quality is not an easy factor to measure or even observe, especially in education which is difficult to evaluate anyway.

In a 1997 study Brian Ray found five variables that had a statistically significant positive impact on home school students' test scores, which are as follows: (1) the education level of the father, (2) the education level of the mother, (3) how many years the child had been home schooled, (4) student gender, and (5) visits to a public library. The problem arises when Ray goes on to report that none of these variables, by themselves or in any combination, explains more than 10 percent of the observed differences in student performance.[16] These five variables may be significant but obviously are not very powerful and furthermore they are not unique. In their 2005 analysis of the Early Childhood Longitudinal Study, Roland Fryer and Steven Levitt found that, of the sixteen variables they tested to explain results on standardized tests for elementary school students, only six had a positive correlation: (1) education level of parents, (2) family socioeconomic status, (3) mother's age at the time of first child's birth, (4) family speaks English, (5) level of parental involvement in PTA, and (6) number of books at home. One factor they tested but was not significant was trips to the museum.[17]

I must make the distinction that Ray was looking for explanatory power for home school student performance, and Fryer and Levitt just examined correlation characteristics of high-achieving students, but even with this caveat there is significant overlap between Ray's variables and Fryer and Levitt's.

Ray tested many other variables, none of which proved to be statistically significant. Besides the five significant variables, Ray also tested teacher certification status of parents, family income, home school budget, family status, time spent in school, and age at which child began school.[18] In other words anything that would make the home school more like a public school is not significant. Combined with the fact that Ray's findings are not unique to home schools and that the variables he did identify were only marginally explanatory, there are some very significant variables that have not been found.

The reason that the key explanatory variables have not been discovered is because the research has had a comparative analysis focus; researchers are looking for characteristic differences between home school students and other students. The factors mentioned earlier miss the key dynamic nature of home schooling as an emerging process as compared to the school model. Home schoolers are different because they are entrepreneurs, something none of the research has examined or researched but home schooling is a different process from public school and that cannot be captured in these sorts of studies.

However, such studies, despite their deficiencies, hint at the key factors such as Ray identifying trips to the library as important. But this looks like Fryer and Levitt's books in the home variable and after all trips to the museum were not significant and that is network building so maybe it is not network building just easy access to reading material. While no one should discount the value of reading, these tests cannot measure if these visits to the museum or library are quality visits or even resulted in more reading. The network building home school family has several advantages the public-school field trip or even the most invested public-school family cannot replicate. The home school family has a high level of schedule flexibility which allows it to visit the library or museum or any place else during low volume hours. This allows for personal attention, the forming of high-quality relationships and greater utilization of the resource or institution. Field trips and museum visits may look similar for public-school and home school students in such studies, but one must get up close to see the significant qualitative differences.

The home school family that goes to the library every week in the middle of the day in the middle of the week when it is lightly used gets to know the library staff and gets personal attention. Since no one else is around the home school family has a much different experience than the public-school student who may only visit the public library if the school library fails to deliver, and then only after the school day is over when libraries often get very busy and very loud and personal attention is not possible. Home school families have not only brought these institutions into their networks but have brought them in at a higher quality level than is even possible for the public-school family without extraordinary and costly effort. This creates a different experience which may be small as a one-time event but accumulates into significant advantages over time.

Another important difference is that many of the services that home school families get through their networks, public schools provide in-house. Public-school students not only participate in music, athletics, and arts outside of school but also participate in these through school programs. This creates an insular affect and restricts the public-school student's socialization, all of the student's life is focused on the school and there is less time or perceived need for building externally focused networks. The criticism that home school students do not get socialization is really upside down, public-school students get intense socialization of peers but not much else in their daily schedule. Home school students must interact with all age groups and so their socialization is much broader. In her 1994 study April Chatham-Carpenter concludes that

> the home schoolers did have differing opportunities for interaction with contacts than the public-schoolers did in the areas of contact ages, frequency of interaction with contacts, and closeness. The public-schoolers had a slightly, although not significantly, larger network of contacts than the home schoolers. The public-schoolers had significantly more peer (within 2 years of subject's age) contacts than the home schoolers; however, the home schoolers had significantly younger (2+ years younger than subject) contacts than public-schoolers. Overall, the home schoolers had significantly more older contacts than either peer or younger contacts; however, the public-schoolers had significantly more peer contacts than older or younger contacts.[19]

As with all things offered by the school (or government), it is a one-size-fits-all solution with limited customization possible to meet the diverse needs and talents of the many individuals within the student body. Home school students effectively have much more choice and are utilizing it.

The Value of Schedule Flexibility

According to Kirzner one of the keys to successful entrepreneurship is the entrepreneur seeing opportunities for better resource coordination. From the perspective of the home school family the public-school day is wasted resources. The student spends a significant amount of the day in non-instructional activities; the day itself is highly structured as is the school year. In reviewing school day policy in the various states, we get a sense of how much time is spent in non-instructional activities. The average school day nationwide as required by state statutes is 5.2 hours, but the states vary quite a bit with some as short as 3 hours and some as long as 7 hours. Some states that have shorter hour requirements do not actually have fewer hours in school, but their statute excludes counting time spent in activities like lunch, recess, rest time, and the like as part of instructional time. In states with these sorts of exclusions, we find states like Delaware with a 3.5-hour day which "excludes lunch" and 4 hours in New Jersey which "do not include recess or lunch periods" or 4 hours in Utah which "do not include lunch and passing periods" contrasted with Texas' 7 hours which include "recess" and "intermission."[20]

These differences in rules and what qualifies and is counted as a school day implies that there is room for better time coordination in the day. Delaware's 3.5 hours of instruction still means the students are in school 6–7 hours each day but about half that time is not instruction time. This is not to imply that home schools do not also waste time, they do, but the advantages of (much) smaller classes means fewer disruptions and the elimination of activities like transfers between class rooms, the settling down at the start of each class, the early pack ups at the end of each class, and the oft overlooked commute to school and home, these are large and add up over time.

The commute alone is significant, the nature of the American school system makes national statistics on the student commute tricky but "[A] commonly cited standard for one-way length (duration) of school bus rides for elementary children is 30 minutes. In an appalling 85 percent of these rural elementary schools, respondents reported that longest rides exceed this upper limit. Worse still, in 25 percent of these rural schools, longest rides reportedly exceed 60 minutes (the suggested standard for high school students)."[21] Using the 30-minute number, twice a day for 180 school days equates to spending 7.5 (24-hour) days on the school bus each year, expanded over 12 years in public school and that is 90 (24-hour) days, 3 full months, commuting to school. Add this to a conservative estimate, based on the previous data, of 1 hour of non-instruction dead time each school day for 180 days for 12 years, that is another 90 days or 3 months. Between dead time and commuting a child will spend a full school year during his or her school career, really more since I am counting 24-hour days, essentially waiting. If the calculation was for 7-hour school days and not 24-hour days it works out to over 600 school days or over 3 school years—waiting. This is a significant amount of time that has better uses as people are finding out with Covid, one can save a lot of time working or schooling from home. A home school family can skip classes every Friday for 12 years (312 school days) and still spend more time educating and less time waiting than the average public-school student does.

As one interviewed mother stated: "[H]ome-schooling absolutely leaves more time for other activities, more time for perks and more time to let them (children) expand a strength or an interest. . . . Traditionally, spots such as ballet studios and indoor pools were empty between the morning preschool-age classes and the late afternoon lessons for school aged children. Increasing numbers of home school classes are being taught during those in-between hours."[22] This is a simple but powerful competitive advantage for home school families.

The flip side of this is that non-school education institutions (museums, art galleries, etc.) have lumpy demand they cannot influence. Many businesses with lumpy demand, such as restaurants, address it with various pricing strategies to try to smooth it some. Early-bird discounts and matinee pricing at theaters are but a couple of examples. This strategy allows them to manage customer flow and resource utilization better. But education institutions are stuck. The hours of the traditional school day lock them in and they cannot woo more students to visit during the day with any sort of pricing strategy which leaves these places under-utilized much of the time and over utilized for a few hours a day. Home school families take advantage of this reality and bring these businesses and institutions into their educational network purely on the strength of schedule flexibility, that not only allows the institutions to better utilize and smooth some of the lumpiness but also results in a higher quality experience for the student or family, just like wait staff can be more attentive to patrons when there are fewer to serve. These types of institutions do not represent nodes unique to the home school networks: the quality of the connection is the difference.

Another way to reveal these hard-to-see-qualitative differences is by the fact that many of these institutions have developed curricula and special events just for home school students or, as it is sometimes called, "family education opportunities." While there is no central collection of data, a perusal of museum websites, as one example, shows that many have developed home school programs like the Heard Museum in Texas:

> Introduce your student to the Natural Sciences. Students will experience learning through classroom activities, outdoor field investigations, laboratory science, small group activities and take-home study packets. Each course curriculum is developed by the Heard Museum's education staff who strive to recognize and meet the needs of homeschool families. All curricula are based on current scientific theory.
>
> Homeschool Science Program is appropriate for children ages 5-12. (Please use child's birthday as of September 1, 2007.) Classes meet 1 day a week for 2 hours from 1–3 P.M.[23]

This program, which is just one of thousands around the country offered by all sorts of institutions, exemplifies how institutions are responding to home schools; it is specifically designed for home school students and is held while public school is in session.

Home school families have effectively brought a wide variety of education providers into their networks ranging from museums and libraries to music instructors and even amusement parks which is allowing them to provide a high-quality education, but flexibility is not the only advantage home school families have.

Customization

The other main home school advantage is the ability parents have to customize and individualize the education program for each child. For the high-investing dissatisfied parent this advantage is key: the ability to break away from the bureaucratic and industrial approach and move away from the median is significant.

The public-school system curriculum is chosen, faculty hired, administrators selected, and goals established with the expectation that the entire organization will march forward through the school year at a certain pace arriving at the set goals at the set time having lost as few students as possible. A public-school student may choose a certain path in high school (academic, general, vocation, etc.), but after that must sign up for the predetermined classes and while some electives are allowed, they are limited. There are attempts within the public system to customize some with specialized schools for the arts or sciences and other disciplines but these schools are few, have highly restrictive admissions policies, and much of the academic curriculum is still determined by the educational bureaucracy.

Regardless of the school's focus, the physical representations of the school are telling: the single file line and the ringing bells, both indicate orderliness and organizational structure. These are some of the same visual and audio representations as the assembly line, factory floor, and prison. Such approaches have their place and function and can facilitate the accomplishment of certain goals, but are far more about orderly standardization and cannot accommodate customization or the individual very well if at all. For example, the Commonwealth of Virginia recently ended its advanced math programs. This approach can lower costs and increase predictability of outcomes and while low costs are always welcomed, predictable uniform outcomes for children with differing talents and interests is exactly the opposite of what the high-investing parent seeks. If a parent wants a customized education tailored to his or her child's individual talents then the satisfaction level with the public system will be low and there will be strong incentives to find or create an alternative.

The difference between the public system and home schooling demonstrates the difference between an ordered top-down bureaucratic system and a bottom-up emergent order. Home schools as individuals or even as a group are not a system, but an emerging order. Public schools look very similar to each other; they have familiar architecture and layout, a similar rhythm and feel and even smell similarly. Each home school looks and is different. There is no centrally determined set of goals and each successful home school is built around what works and what has not worked in achieving those goals, which are also individualistic. Each home school has some experimentation, some trial and error in building its network, and finding the resources that best helps it achieve its ultimate goals. In public school the student must adapt to the school's way of doing things; success is defined by how well the student navigates and manages the school's system. In a successful home school, the school adapts to the student.

An Out-of-Date Model

It is not that schools do not want to serve all the students, they do. Public schools are full of dedicated teachers and staff. It is not that they do not try to offer variety: schools regularly have guest speakers, go on field trips, and sponsor extracurricular activities. But, the public-school system, despite any other notions and wishes to the contrary, is a government agency. It is more like the Internal Revenue Service or motor vehicles administration than most supporters want to admit; it cannot be flexible because it cannot deviate too much for fear of getting outside of the solution set and creating a political imbalance. Like most government programs and agencies, it has to be mostly a one-size-fits-all bureaucracy with limited and minimal deviation. The public-school system is unable to respond to market pressures. It cannot, in any way, handle the doubling of knowledge on a daily basis. In fact, not only can it not respond, it is insulated from the market and designed to *not* be responsive to the market but to the politicians and the ballot box. This reality means that customization and creativity are expensive, risky, and not well rewarded; and when those three conditions exist there will not be much creativity.

When information was much more difficult to obtain and costly the school model made sense and many communities formed schools that frequently met in the local church, sometimes taught by the local pastor and many times by a hired teacher. This socialization of the costs by either voluntary association or, later, state compulsion, effectively lowered the cost of obtaining education for the individual demander. In these early years the school was very responsive to the community as each school served a small community and the parents were very much and directly involved. However, as this community approach evolved into the bureaucratic approach and schools became government agencies parents were less directly involved and schools became insulated from the community and more beholden to politicians. But at the same time, information has become much less costly with the advent of a vibrant publishing industry, the development of electronic media and eventually the internet, and modern communications the cost of obtaining information and education has dramatically decreased. Kirzner argues that firms that do not adjust to decreasing costs risk being replaced by entrepreneurial activity: "[F]or me the function of the entrepreneur consists not of shifting the curves of cost or of revenues which face him, but of noticing that they have in fact shifted."[24] The educational entrepreneurs known as home schoolers are responding to their dissatisfaction but their particular response is made possible by the fact that cost curves have shifted and the public schools have not responded to this and have actually become more expensive as the cost of information and knowledge has decreased dramatically. Educational entrepreneurs have capitalized on these developments by building individual resource and information networks, and establishing various markets in which expertise and information is traded, none of which existed or was possible twenty-five years ago.

The question now is, how are they doing? A question I address in the next chapter.

NOTES

1. Education: Teaching Children at Home 1978.
2. Education: Teaching Children at Home 1978.
3. Medlin, Homeschooling and the quesrion of socialization 2000, 110–111.
4. Goff, Learning with Friends 2003.
5. Kirzner 1973, 68.
6. HEDUA.Com 2012.
7. HEDUA.Com 2012.
8. Hayek, The Use of Knowledge in Society 1945, 1.
9. HEDUA.Com 2012.
10. Alonso-Cortes, Trade and Language: Adam Smith's Rhetoric of Persuasion 2008, 1.
11. Coase, The Nature of the Firm 1937.
12. These estimates are based on Buckminster Fuller's Knowledge Doubling Curve which has been extended and revised since Fuller's death. Available at many places including https://learningsolutionsmag.com/articles/2468/marc-my-words-the-coming-knowledge-tsunami.
13. Wikipedia n.d.
14. Kirzner 1973.
15. HEDUA.Com 2012.

16. B. Ray 1997, 79–81.
17. Fryer and Levitt, The Black-White Test Score Gap Through Third Grade 2006.
18. B. Ray 1997.
19. Chatham-Carpenter 1994.
20. Colasanti 2007.
21. Howley 2001.
22. Goff, Learning with Friends 2003.
23. For more information about the program at the Heard Museum its website may be visited at http://www.heardmuseum.org/attractions/individual.asp.
24. Kirzner 1973, 81.

Chapter 5

Home School Investment and Profits

The goal of schooling is to educate the next generation and to teach them what they need to know and how to think about new things they will encounter in life. Since time and resources are scarce, teaching involves making some very difficult choices. Education is about trying to prepare a person for his or her future when no one knows what that will be.

There are other problems as well. Education is a long-term project and it is years after the fact before anyone knows if the education was proper and useful. Plus, the causal relationship between education and life success is tenuous and indirect at best; we can get millionaires, great humanitarians, and criminals not only from the same school but from the same family. But these issues notwithstanding, we should over the population and through time see some evidence that home schooling works or does not. That is, it is providing a better education to students. This is a very subjective measure though. As I tell students, you have to define your terms especially when we use mushy words like fair or better. So, to be consistent and should any of my students read this let me define better.

Better has several definitions. The first is basic and foundational and that is superior academic performance. This can be measured in many ways and I will look at several. The second definition is longer-term life success, and the third is determining if home school graduates' are positive social contributors. There are many aspects we could examine and I will expand and explain these in more detail along the way but it should be remembered that another way to measure better is getting the same results with a much lower investment. Better can also mean that parents and students are just happier and more satisfied. Furthermore, home schoolers have other goals beside a better education that need to be considered as well.

Chapter 5

HOME SCHOOLING: THE INVESTMENT

Home schooling is difficult, and it is undoubtedly true that some parents run into more difficulties than they anticipate. Studies show there is a drop-off in the number of children home schooled as they reach high-school age. There are many reasons for this drop-off but it raises a basic question as to whether home schooling is a truly viable educational approach or just some parents acting out in frustration to the public system's deficiencies or wanting to play school and then giving up when it gets harder. I expect there is some of that, but successful home schooling is a serious commitment and requires some investment. However, many of the costs, critics and other researchers often reference, are not really as relevant as they first seem as successful families have found ways to minimize them.

What's a High-investing Parent to Do?

Before examining specific costs, it is important to understand the choices and potential payoffs for parents. There are essentially two kinds of parents to consider the high-investing parent and the low-investing parent. We have already assumed all parents want the best education possible in our previous discussion on the solution set but that does not mean all parents invest the same. The choice for parents is: What is the best outcome given the investment they are willing to make?

A high-investing parent, and by this, I mean they are going to be a persistent and active participant in the child's education, must consider where they will realize the best return on that investment. If a parent decided to leave his child in the public school, high investing may mean spending money but almost definitely means spending time with the child, with the teachers at the school attending meetings, and being very active in all things school. A parent can choose to stay in the public school and visit the school, attend PTA meetings, get active with the school-board elections, maybe even run for the office himself, chaperone field trips and dances, help with fundraisers, review homework every night, hire outside tutors, and get involved in every way possible. This would be a considerable amount of effort and investment, and a large amount of research (Ziegler 1987, Eagle 1989, Henderson and Berla 1994, and Carey, Lewis and Farris 1994) shows that this sort of parental involvement will improve a child's academic performance. Recall from the previous chapter that Fryer and Levitt found parental involvement in PTA to be positively correlated with student performance.[1] It is not that going to meetings with teachers and other parents helps the student do better but the parent who will go to meetings is investing in the child's education in other ways as well.

But some or much of that investment is lost or wasted. The investment will help the student but any investment in trying to improve the school will be largely dissipated by the school bureaucracy. And then the parent may feel the school and they are against each other. It is one thing to help a student with troubling assignments; it is another if the parents think the assignment incorrect, incomplete, or otherwise inadequate in some way. A parent can help with the former but cannot do much with the latter. The advocacy for parental involvement tends to be a one-way relationship, with the school system expecting the parent to help the student accomplish what the school has assigned, there is very little in the way of the school helping the parent accomplish something the parent wants, parents are to defer to the experts and support their efforts. If a parent of a school student (public or private) is not happy with his child's history curriculum the probability of getting it changed is almost zero and the probability of getting it changed in time to impact his child is absolutely zero. The most likely result, if the parent is alone or represents a small minority of voices, is that nothing will change. If the parent gathers enough support to be successful in effecting change, that takes time and a significant amount of effort and then the proposed change must still work its way through the bureaucracy and faces many points for rejection or compromise. This is intentional. A school system is a bureaucracy with a solution set designed to resist exogenous shocks, it is too risky to the political balance between interest groups. Such things as an effective activist parent group or a complete philosophical turnover in the school board is resisted by the pre-established rules and the bureaucratic momentum of previous decisions as well as counter pressures applied by the other interest groups.

Contrast this process to a home school parent who is not happy with a curriculum, he buys a new one this week. The change is not costless, but it is complete and immediate. Recall the entrepreneurial characteristic of needing control: this is one of the most important things a parent can control; educational content. The parent may continue to experiment and search for the right resources or right relationship to meet his child's needs which are ever changing as he or she moves through school and matures. In a practical sense while the high-investing public-school parent may help his child perform better, the parent has little if any control over the child's education, the child is still learning to merely master the median education.

A high-investing parent has to consider where the best return is; in large bureaucratic organizations with large classes or in starting his own educational enterprise called a home school. Educational researchers McKenzie and Staaf (1970) point out that each child has different academic endowments and that even in a two-student class the education product will not be ideal for either student, and teacher efforts to improve this will be severely limited by the needs of the other student(s).[2] The median education is not just at the organizational and policy level but filters right down to what is taught in each classroom. The more students in a class the less likely the education being offered will meet any but the most basic needs but it only takes two students in a class for this compromise to have its impact. Even if the parent is not concerned about the organizational resistance to changing and adapting to new conditions and is willing to highly invest in his child by aiding and supplementing the education the school offers, he will find some of his investment will go toward customizing and adapting the median education of each class to suit his child better. In effect he will be creating a home school light.

Beyond the investment level, a parent must decide which educational method, school or home school, is best. Obviously, this is more of a sliding scale but the distinction has value for the analysis. For this analysis, any sort of school model is essentially the same: private schools may be more responsive to parents but no individual parent has a high probability of effecting immediate and significant changes. This results in four possible outcomes which can be summarized in a two-by-two matrix with the expected payoffs from each combination in the corresponding boxes as shown in table 5.1.

A high-investing parent faces the reality that the school system, either by design or incidentally, wastes some portion of his investment and will leave him with a lower-net return. That there is a real and costly trade-off between less parental control and influence in favor of deferring to experts and school resources. If a parent wants a unique, non-median education, high investing in the school system will be expensive and frustrating, or both. The control and influence to provide a non-median education are only available in a home school where the high-investing parent can realize significant gains since all of their investment flows directly to the child's education and is not dissipated or resisted by bureaucracy and interest group competition.

However, the school model is a good deal for low-investing parents, they get all the benefits of the school resources and are not looking to add much to it, so they get a median return for no additional investment. The socialized setting of a school not only limits the gains of the high-investing parent but also minimizes the losses of the low investor. It moves everyone toward the median. There is a sense that that is what school officials expect and think of parents. While certainly not proof that all school officials think this way a "hot-mic" moment in a California school-board meeting on February 20, 2021, illustrates this point well.

> Oakley Unified Elementary School District board members were caught making disparaging comments about parents during a virtual meeting Wednesday that they believed was private. Before the meeting officially began, board members talked about parents who have complained about children still in distance

Table 5.1 School Methodology Choice-Effort Payoff Matrix

School Choice Investment Level	Home School	Traditional School
High Investment	Large net private gains	Minimal net private gains
Low Investment	Large net private losses	Significant net private gains

learning. At one point, board member Kim Beede asked the group if they were the only ones in the meeting before she used profanity. Lisa Brizendine said parents often forget that board members are also parents and community members when writing letters complaining about school re-openings. "They don't know what goes on behind the scenes and it's really unfortunate they want to pick on us because they want their babysitters back," Brizendine said.[3]

This shows a school bureaucracy not wanting parental involvement and a view that parents are low investors in their children's education. The parents were outraged and started a petition and the school superintendent apologized and several board members resigned but one wonders how it would have been handled had it not been made public after all, no other school-board member called Brizendine out and several expressed agreements with her comments. But the point that the community outcry overlooked is that, inflammatory comments aside, most of the eight-minute video was the board discussing how some other school boards had technology to limit parental input by setting up a phone message system that cuts off parental comments after three minutes when they call in to the school-board comment line. Every member of the Oakley school board wanted this system which is obviously in place elsewhere.[4] Everything in the eight minutes was either about how to minimize high-investor parental involvement or disparaging low-investor parents.

However low-investing parent is setting up for failure if they choose to home school. It takes dedication to make an entrepreneurial effort a success; it is not for the low-level investor. Some critics tacitly agree with this analysis by arguing that home schooling removes the most active and involved parents from the public-school system.

> Home schooling . . . undermines the common good in two ways. First, it withdraws not only children but also social capital from public-schools, to the detriment of the students remaining behind. Second, as an exit strategy, home schooling undermines the ability of public education to improve and become more responsive as a democratic institution. Thus, home schooling is not only a reaction to, but also a cause of, declining public-schools. Therefore,

it diminishes the potential of public education to serve the common good in a vibrant democracy.[5]

This is a very romantic notion of what public schools do especially since school systems do not encourage and certainly do not (cannot) reward high-investing parents. High-investing parents are a threat to the solution set and risks upsetting the political balance, it is why school boards install phone lines that cut parents off. A rational high-investing parent will try to invest in a way that has the best potential return.

Years before home schooling became popular, McKenzie and Staaf (1970), in their own way, identify this high-investing–low-investing issue. "Students could obtain their desired (education) bundle if they hired separate tutors; however, the resulting satisfaction is offset by the economy that a classroom arrangement permits."[6] They capture much in this little statement, students and parents are dissatisfied and there are better solutions which involve individualized education bundles that will create higher satisfaction. But this response is expensive. The school advantage in 1970, when they wrote, were the economies of scale. They are making the Coase argument that the firm approach made sense in 1970 because transactions costs to obtaining knowledge and teaching it were high. If relative prices changed, as they have, then the classroom arrangement becomes relatively more expensive and should be replaced by an alternative, in 1970 that looked like private tutoring which would certainly be a high investment. But now it looks like home schooling and some students are obtaining their desired education bundle. This is still a high investment but much more obtainable than private tutors.

Home School Costs: Which Costs Count?

As home school entrepreneurs consider their options, costs are a very important part of the decision process. But the few analyses that look at the costs of home schooling do not really dig into the details and make certain assumptions that do not hold for most home schooling parents.

While it varies by region and by state, the national average spending per pupil in the public-school system is $12,612 per year for a K–12 education. The highest costing region is the Northeast with New York predictably the most expensive state at $24,040. The least costing region is the South, although the West and Midwest are not much higher and Utah is the lowest-cost state at $7,628 per pupil.[7] However, when test scores are compared such as the National Assessment of Education Progress exams some high-spending states such as Massachusetts, New Jersey, and New Hampshire do well but so do some low-spending states such as South Dakota, Montana, and Wyoming, and the same is true for low performers which include both high-spending and low-spending states.[8] It is interesting that for eighth-grade math (one of many measures available) the highest spending state, New York, averaged a score of 280 out of 500 and lowest spending state, Utah, averaged 281. The national average is 280.[9]

These costs are not unimportant; they serve as indicators of how costly the old approach to education is with its expensive infrastructure and staff of highly trained experts and administrators. This is a piece of information that home school families would consider but these costs are sunk. No one gets to pay lower taxes by withdrawing their children from the school system (a few states do offer some small tax relief for home school families) or when their children graduate, this is a socialized cost that every taxpayer pays for his or her entire life. This public school per pupil cost is relevant in answering the question about how much will it cost to educate a child but that is where its relevance ends. The costs that are vital for a home school family to consider are the additional costs that will be incurred, those are the costs that needed to change and/or be noticed to make home schooling viable.

Counting the True Costs: Investing in Home Schooling

Accounting for and detailing costs and benefits is tricky business; it is easy to count things that should not be and omit things that should be included. There are a collection of costs that some include as a cost of home schooling that should not be included because they are not uniquely related to home schooling. With this in mind, the costs can be grouped into three categories: (1) the loss of income, (2) the opportunity cost of time, and (3) additional expenditures.

Second Earner Income: How Much Is Truly Lost?

Potentially, the largest cost is the lost income of having a spouse stay at home to teach and not in compensated employment. This obviously varies by family and situation but it is safe to assume that, on average, the non-working spouse, if employed, might earn an income of tens of thousands of dollars annually. Using education level as a proxy for income earning potential I can derive an estimate of how much income may be forgone. Home school parents have the same education attainment as the general population, for example 45 percent of home school parents have a college degree or higher and 44 percent of the general population does,[10] it is safe to assume that, on average, the non-working spouse could command the national median income and it would be logical to assume that this is a significant opportunity cost to home schooling. However, home school families have taken various steps to minimize this cost and, in many cases, the notion of a lost income may not be as significant as it first seems.

Overwhelmingly, the teaching spouse is a stay-at-home mother.[11] This is significant. For almost every occupation (for a variety of reasons that are beyond the scope of this book) women earn less than men. Daniel Wienberg, assistant director of the census, studied the earnings data from the 2000 U.S. census. He reported in his *Earnings by Gender: Evidence from Census 2000* that in all but a few of the 505 occupations he studied men earn more:

> The highest paid occupation for men and for women is *physicians and surgeons*, but the female median in this occupation ($88,000) is but 63 percent that of the male median ($140,000). Fifteen of the listed occupations for men also appear on the list for women, and in all cases, the female median is less than that for men. In fact, the occupation that is third on the list for women (*dentists*) makes about the same ($68,000) as the occupation that is last on the list for men (*management analysts,* $67,000).
>
> A similar pattern is shown for the lowest paid occupations. Sixteen occupations appear on both lists, and in all cases but one (*dining room and cafeteria attendants and bartender helpers*), women make less than men in the same occupation. In only five occupations with 10,000 or more workers are female median earnings at least 100 percent of male median earnings.[12]

Subsequent work makes similar findings:

> The gender gap in pay has narrowed since 1980, but it has remained relatively stable over the past 15 years or so. In 2018, women earned 85 percent of what men earned, according to a Pew Research Center analysis of median hourly earnings of both full- and part-time workers in the United States. Based on this estimate, it would take an extra 39 days of work for women to earn what men did in 2018.[13]

So, home school families choose to make the lower earning spouse the teacher but there are more factors to consider; what if the wife/mother would have never been in the workforce? "Marital status matters for women's labor force participation. Below age forty-five, married women are noticeably less likely to work than single women."[14] If home schooling mothers were not going to join the labor force anyway, and data suggests there is an even chance of that being the case, then it would be incorrect to count their lost income as a cost of home schooling. Munnell and Zhivan noted in their research that for all age groups, married women were less likely to be in the labor force during their prime child-bearing years. Almost 40 percent of women aged twenty-five through thirty-four were not in the labor force.[15] They go on to report that women with small children are even less likely to be in the work force; "The labor force participation of wives increases directly with the age of their children. Only slightly more than half of married women with children under 3 were in the labor force in 2004 compared to 79 percent for their counterparts with children aged 14 to 17."[16] Forty-nine percent of home school families have three children or more, which is a decrease from earlier years when 60 percent of home school families had three or more children.[17] But this translates into the mother having more years of children under the age of three and being more likely to stay home even in the absence of home schooling. Assuming these statistics translate to home school families then losing a second income is not a consideration for about half the families.

Even if choosing to home school did not cause half the families to sacrifice a second income, it still leaves the other half that could and probably would have had an employed mother if they had not chosen to home school. For these families, it is appropriate to count that lost income. Given that the family demographics and education profile of home school mothers does not vary much from the general population, it is safe to assume that the salaries of home school mothers in the work force are distributed similarly to other employed women. The median salary for working women in 2018 was $45,097.[18]

However, an often-overlooked aspect of this analysis is that entering the workforce comes with some significant costs as well, offsetting the second earner's disposable income. These are some factors even non-home school families need to consider. It is expensive to have a second earner:

> According to 2019 data from Salary.com, if you are a stay-at-home mom (or dad), and were paid for your services, you would be looking at a median annual salary of $178,201. Why? Because many stay-at-home parents work around the clock. If you have young children, work can often mean nighttime feedings, greeting early morning risers, and late-night meal prep. In addition, a stay-at-home parent wears many hats and must employ many skills in order to be a tutor, negotiator, nurse, party planner, and chef, for starters.[19]

This is a significant amount of value, when mom goes to work some of these valuable services have to be hired out, while some are done less often and less well and some simply forgone. Meanwhile, average federal taxes would be approximately 25 percent or possibly higher and reduce that $45,097 annual income to $33,822. Social security would tax another 7.35 percent away and state income taxes are on average 2.5 percent,[20] leaving a net income after taxes of about $30,500 or about $2,540 a month. After that, any number of other expenses would be incurred, including childcare, work clothing, more meals out, commuting, increases in other taxes, out sourcing

74   Chapter 5

chores like lawn mowing, and much more not to mention the value of time. There are many things to consider, as one mother who is also an accountant wrote when she considered going back to work:

> I was curious exactly how much I would *really* make if I went back to work, so naturally, that called for a new spreadsheet. My calculations tell me that the amount of money I would *actually* have in my pocket from going back to work is approximately 43% of my expected salary. Only forty-three percent! I would basically be working for less than half my pay.[21]

A *Business Week* article details this decision calculation in a sort of day-in-the-life style that makes the trade-offs clear and stark:

> For Nancy McCardel, the days start early. At 5:30 a.m., she gets up to feed her three-month-old daughter before showering and dressing in a blouse and suit ($300, plus $12 a week for dry cleaning). She rouses her 8-year-old son, and during the summer, whisks him off to a day-care center ($112 per week). She then drops off her daughter at another center ($210 per week) across town. She drives downtown to her job ($4 roundtrip, plus $22.50 per week for parking) as managing supervisor for a public relations firm in Atlanta and picks up a gourmet cup of coffee ($3 a day). She eats lunch ($4) at her desk. At 4:30 she races from the office to get the kids. After a quick dinner, she bathes the children, reads to them, tucks them into their freshly made beds ($70 for bimonthly housecleaning), and does chores. By 10:30, she tumbles into bed. At week's end, this thirty-five-year-old wife and mother wonders: Is it worth it?
>
> Financially, the answer isn't clear. Although more than half of all women with preschool children hold paid jobs, many of them soon discover that much of their earnings are eaten up by the costs of child care, a professional wardrobe, and other work-related expenses. Ultimately, some women (and many men) argue it doesn't pay for women to work when the kids are small.
>
> The numbers certainly seem to support that assumption. For example, a hypothetical suburban couple working in New York City and whose combined income is $150,000 saves more than $15,000 in federal taxes, $5,070 in FICA taxes, and $5,184 in state and local taxes when they live on a single income of $80,000. The couple will save an additional $32,634 when they lop off the mother's costs of working: child care, commuting, and such. Instead of losing $70,000 in income, the actual loss is only $4,544.[22]

The article does, in another section, point out that there are long-term benefits to working even when the present marginal income is low, such as experience, promotion, company benefits, and continuation in service that may make it more valuable in the long run for mothers to stay in the workforce.

But the article is clear: mothers working during their children's early years are making an investment in future returns from the job and may just be breaking even or losing in the short term.

A reduced estimated loss of disposable income changes the analysis of the decision but even this small income loss may not be the full story. In reality the home school family may not be giving up any net income at all. The home school teacher is not only a teacher. As pointed out before, there is great flexibility in home schooling and this flexibility allows time for income generation. Ray reported that about 16 percent of home school mothers work outside the home;[23] the National Center of Education Statistics, the Coalition for Responsible Home Education,[24] and the Fraser Institute all found that approximately a quarter to a third of home school mothers are in the work force at least part time.[25] The HEDUA survey found 12 percent of parents worked part time from home and 15 percent worked full time from home.[26] If some income can be generated without incurring many of the attendant costs of a two-income family, many home school families may not be sacrificing much income at all and some may actually, on net, have higher earnings. If a third of home school mothers earn income and assuming that half the home school families would have had a stay-at-home mother anyway, then it can be concluded that the number of families truly sacrificing a second income is relatively small, around 20 percent of all home school families and, what they are sacrificing on net while not insignificant is a proportionally small amount of income; maybe not much more than $5,000 of annual disposable income.

Time Is Money

The opportunity cost of time is the second consideration. Even if a mother planned to stay home, choosing to home school changes the way she uses her time each day. The value of the forgone income should be considered a minimum value of a mother's time since a stay-at-home mother has already decided her time is more valuable than her potential earnings. Potentially, there are myriad of options available for how she might use her time while the children were in school, ranging from self-improvement to recreation, to employment, to chores, to more time with the preschool aged children, social activities to volunteer work, and much more.

It is accurate to consider a less-kept home or the forgoing of the acquisition of a new skill as a real cost of home schooling but it is difficult to quantify these sorts of costs. We know leisure time (defined as any time not spent in compensated employment) is valuable and can have a high opportunity cost so it is proper to include it in this discussion. Much of the literature estimates leisure time at the forgone wage rate but the calculation is more difficult for the non-employed. Economists Peter Feather and Douglas Shaw have developed models estimating the value of leisure time. An estimate that has emerged from their research is $19 an hour. When adjusting for certain variables the value of leisure time of a non-working mother with some college education is approximately $15 an hour.[27] This estimate may appear low, but it translates to $30,000 (8-hour days for 52 weeks) a year and exceeds the estimate of net earnings from work of $5–10,000 a year, as economic theory would predict the value of leisure time is greater than the value of work.

However, it is not all as it seems. If a non-home schooling parent decides to be a stay-at-home spouse, it is not like they suddenly have eight hours a day to pursue that hobby, take a spa day, build that new table, or learn French. Recall the $178,201 estimate of the value of the services provided by stay-at-home spouses, stay-at home spouses are busy. That spouse will spend time doing many tasks the family needs done, not the least of which are numerous tasks tied to the school and its schedule. Dropping children off and picking them up, after-school events, parent-teacher conferences, taking the forgotten homework or lunch to school are all part of a week already filled with other household tasks. A report from the Bureau of Labor Statistics gives some insight on how a typical day goes:

> Adults living in households with children under age six spent an average of 2.2 hours per day providing primary childcare to household children. Adults living in households where the youngest child was between the ages of six and seventeen spent less than half as much time providing primary childcare to household children—48 minutes per day. . . . On an average day in 2019, among adults living with children under age 6, those who were not employed spent about an hour more caring for and helping household children than did employed adults—2.8 hours versus 1.7 hours. Adults living in households with at least one child under age six spent an average of 5.4 hours per day providing secondary childcare—that is, they had at least one child in their care while doing activities other than primary childcare.[28]

Children's ages make a difference but stay-at-home spouses spend a lot of time doing child care already and add to that that these are educationally high-investing parents and as time in direct care diminishes time spent helping with homework and other school-related activities would increase. Time spent helping with homework was not included in the survey but other research reports that the average American parent spends 6.2 hours a week helping with homework[29] and since home school parents are high investors, the 6.2 should be thought of as a floor.

Depending on the age and number of children a stay-at-home spouse's day may not leave much time for those French lessons and spa days (which is no surprise to any parent) and we can safely assume and while $30,000 may seem a low estimate on the value of leisure time it really is more of a potential upper limit. The best use of time is addressing those tasks valued at $178,000. Due to these valuable demands on parents' time, the actual figure for personal leisure time is significantly lower. Obviously, each family has their own valuation of what this is worth but for high-investing parents who are already committed to spending as many hours in school work as necessary the cost in time to transition from a high-investing public-school parent to a home school parent is relatively low: "one might infer that if normal parents help their child with homework an average of 6.7 hours per week (the global average), then they are already giving their child the equivalent of two days of homeschool per week."[30] This assumes the average home school day is three to four hours and based on some casual observations of home school internet chat rooms it may be accurate, it is certainly logical although we have no reliable data. The overall point is true, high-investing public-school parents already *are* home schooling part time but as volunteers of the public system, beholden to its curriculum and approach.

Direct Costs

The third item to discuss is the out-of-pocket expenses. This is the shortest section because it is the most straightforward and needing the least explanation. This includes the purchase of curricula, dues to join home school groups, co-op fees, tutors, and the other unique items necessary to home educate a child. The amount home school families spend on education related expenses varies greatly. While there are some outliers, estimates in several studies put the upper range at around $2,500 annually for the first child and slightly less for following children.[31] One study frequently cited puts the range between $700 and $1,800 per student[32] and this is broadly consistent with numerous reports such as a recent one out of Minnesota that put the range spend between $300 and $1,000 per family each year[33] and the HEDUA survey which reported that 72 percent of families spend between $300 and $1,000 per child per year.[34]

The Bottom Line on Costs

So, in the end, what does it cost, or from another perspective what is the required investment, to home educate a child? Obviously, the answer depends, but that is one of the great advantages of home schooling, the parents can choose and invest the exact amount they want for each child, subject to the family budget constraint. But, these sorts of analyses seem unfinished without providing some sort of number. We can say that for a family with one child and a spouse who would have worked the net costs could be quite high;

with lost earnings and lost leisure time it may cost $50,000 a year or more. On the other hand, for a family with three or four children with a spouse who was going to stay home anyway or whose job was a small net contributor to family income it is accurate to assume that the direct costs are the only costs that really matter and that family could home school all children for approximately $3,000 a year. What is known is that each family choosing to home school has decided that it looks worth it and those that stick with it have concluded it definitely is.

SO WHICH COST CURVES SHIFTED?

If, as I am arguing, the proper analytical framework for understanding home schooling is the Kirznerian entrepreneur and the Kirznerian entrepreneur is alert to changing costs, then we should be able to identify which costs have changed. So, which of these cost curves have shifted? The answer is all of them to some extent.

In the labor market it is much less costly to not be a full-time worker. This may seem counterintuitive given the steady drum beat we hear in some quarters about needing two incomes to make ends meet and how poorly middle-class wages have done over the last thirty or forty years. But if we look at the labor market from a slightly different perspective another story emerges. Since 1950 real family median income has more than doubled but during that time male labor force participation has declined from 86 percent to 70 percent while female participation increased until 1999 and has been in gradual decline since.[35] In one sense being out of the workforce is costlier since incomes are higher but, in another sense, since workers are more productive, if a family aspires to a certain lifestyle it is easier to reach it than it was a few decades ago.

This is seen in real measurable material progress, for example, people have larger homes. In the 1950s the average home was 983 square feet, leaving about 292 square feet per person.[36] Today the average home is 2,392 square feet leaving 924 square feet per person.[37] Today's houses have almost as much room per person as the entire house size in the 1950s; houses are more than twice as large but of course square footage is not the entire story; dishwashers and washing machines and dryers and climate control and garbage disposals all make the house not just larger but better. Families have more cars, travel more, have more leisure time, have more education, and so much more. The point here is not to argue that life is materially better; it is, but to argue that this betterment makes it less costly to a family's lifestyle to operate on a single income, that a reasonable lifestyle can be maintained on the household median income, which home school families achieve despite the fact that home school families are less likely to have two parents in the workforce. Public-school families have a 9 percent higher rate of two-earner families than home school families yet they have similar income demographics with 81 percent being above poverty for both groups. Private-school student families are much wealthier.[38] Furthermore, the HEDUA survey found that their median income was $71,500[39] at a time when the median household income in the United States was $56,912.[40]

The main costs that truly shifted are the direct costs. Obtaining the materials and other education resources has become much easier and much less expensive with the growth in home schooling and the advent of the internet. One small example, mentioned earlier, of how these costs have changed is the *Encyclopedia Britannica* which cost $1,400 the last year it was printed (2012) for the full 32-volume set and is now available for $70 as an annual subscription for the online version. That is a significant decrease in the cost of knowledge for what was once considered the best and most comprehensive collection of knowledge and facts in the world. But, even before the internet as the number of home schooling families increased the education market responded by offering all sorts of material besides the traditional expensive textbooks. Home school fairs and expos large and small provided the infrastructure for a vibrant secondary market as well as primary market for educational materials. In addition to professional publishers offering products tailored to this new market, many home school parents developed their own material for their own use and then offered them for sale as well. In the 2012 HEDUA survey parents were asked about how they obtained curriculum and the answers show this diversity; in addition to online (94 percent) and retail stores (25 percent), 73 percent report purchasing used materials, 32 percent borrow materials from friends, 55 percent purchase materials at a home school convention, and 10 percent do something else as well.[41] In the same survey the 81 percent of the parents report they spend less than $1,000 per child and 50 percent spend less than $500 per child per year.[42] Meanwhile, public-school "[F]amilies with students in grades one through 12 plan to spend a per-student average of $696.70 on back-to-school supplies in 2019, according to a recent survey by the National Retail Federation, America's biggest retail trade group."[43]

The high-investing parent is facing the prospect of investing thousands of dollars in time and money in back-to-school supplies, homework help and meetings to help the student adapt to the schools' curriculum and teaching style only to see some of that investment dissipated by the social and bureaucratic nature of the school. Furthermore, the parents have to deal with a school administration that may be less than anxious to have high-investing parental involvement anyway. Facing that prospect, it can be very rational to sacrifice a marginal increase in material well-being to start a home school. But the question is, are they earning a profit?

PROFIT MAXIMIZATION: THE RIGHT ANALYSIS?

Standard microeconomic analysis assumes that firms have a goal to maximize profits, and successful firms accomplish this goal in the long run. But business profits and losses are relatively easy to measure and see, and we have accounting processes that track and measure business activity and get an answer. Home schoolers do not have these measures of success or failure available to them. But, for the entrepreneur analysis to hold there must be some measure akin to profits. Educational entrepreneurs have to have some notion of success or profit since some home schoolers home school all their children for their entire education while others abandon their home schooling along the way. Some abandons may be planned, according to one relatively recent survey about a fifth of home school families do not intend to school into high school, but 80 percent do.[44] Earlier surveys were a little different. Ray's 1997 survey reported that the mean grade level through which parents intended to home educate was 11.83, or essentially all the way through high school.[45] But that same study showed a significant drop in home school participation between the eighth and ninth grades.[46] Rudner's 1999 study confirms Ray's findings that there was a significant drop between eighth and ninth grades.[47] So while the parents may have intended to home school through high school the situation at the time of the study was that many high-school students were headed off to some sort of school. However, in a 2004 follow-up study Ray shows a much smaller and more gradual drop-off by the twelfth grade.[48] Rudner's theory that the "Possible reasons for this lower participation for high-school students may be the relative newness of the home-school movement, early graduation from high school, and possibly a desire on the part of some homeschool parents to enroll their children in a traditional high school"[49] may have some validity here; five years after his first study, Ray was looking at a more mature and knowledgeable home school market. In addition to these considerations about profit, home school parents change curricula, move their students to new grades and material, advance them into new classes, and eventually graduate them, all of which require some idea of what success or failure looks like.

But how does one measure this? Home schoolers face a different challenge, really a two-pronged challenge; the problems with providing a quality education, the network building and customization as discussed in the previous chapter and then the problem of determining if what they are doing is achieving their goals.

Even though I am describing educational entrepreneurs as Kirzerian entrepreneurs, Kirzner does not provide a satisfactory definition of profits for my purposes. Kirzner's entrepreneur is more of an arbitrageur, finding price differences in markets and exploiting them.[50] Home schoolers are doing this in finding underused resources like empty museums during the school day and making them more valuable by utilizing them and while that activity is a vitally important process, it is not a measure of how well the student is doing.

For a better definition I turn to Ludwig von Mises:

> Profit, in a broader sense, is the gain derived from action; it is the increase in satisfaction (decrease in uneasiness) brought about; it is the difference between the higher value attached to the result attained and the lower value attached to the sacrifices made for its attainment; it is, in other words, yield minus cost. To make profit is invariably the aim sought by any action. If an action fails to attain the ends sought, yield either does not exceed costs or lags behind costs. In the latter case, the outcome means a loss, a decrease in satisfaction.
>
> Profit and loss in this original sense are psychic phenomena and as such not open to measurement and a mode of expression which could convey to other people precise information concerning their intensity. A man can tell a fellow man that *a* suits him better than *b*; but he can not communicate to another man, except in vague and indistinct terms, how much the satisfaction derived from *a* exceeds that derived from *b*.[51]

Kirzner's profit is consistent with Mises', and Kirzner is motivated by Mises in many ways, but Kirzner's definition is much narrower. Mises' definition is a more useful framework for discussing educational entrepreneurial profit that consists of a bundle of outcomes, some of which have objective measures and some that are more subjective but which certainly fit the concept of increased satisfaction or decreased uneasiness, a key notion for the dissatisfied parent.

What Are the Home School Goals?

This analysis must start with understanding why home school families make this choice, what are their goals. Despite what some critics assume, families are not undertaking this difficult task for any single reason. Home schoolers are not a monolith but there are some consistent answers that emerge in different studies. Table 5.1 presents the results from several different studies.

Aside from these surveys, there have been some in-depth studies into this issue as well. In their 2007 study, Basham, Merrifield, and Hepburn found that the most commonly cited advantages articulated by both Canadian and U.S. parents were as follows:

- the opportunity to impart a particular set of values and beliefs;
- higher academic performance through one-on-one instruction;
- the opportunity to develop closer and stronger parent-child relationships;
- the opportunity for the child to experience high-quality interaction with peers and adults;
- the lack of discipline in public schools;

- the opportunity to escape negative peer pressure (e.g., drugs, alcohol, and premarital sex) through controlled and positive social interactions;
- the expense of private schools; and
- a physically safer environment in which to learn.[52]

While Basham, Merrifield, and Hepburn described the previous list as advantages it is really a list of goals. The choice to home school does not instantly make the items listed come about; home schooling just provides parents the opportunity to achieve these goals. Their findings are consistent across a variety of studies including Bauman (2002, 2001), Bielick, Chandler, and Broughman (2001), and Ray (2001). For example, in 2004 Ray found the top reasons home school parents cited for their choice were in this order:

- to provide a better education;
- to provide preferred religious instruction;
- to provide family's values;
- to develop student's character;
- public-school teachings were objectionable;
- better learning environment at home; and
- to gain more child parent interactions.[53]

Education entrepreneurs invest to achieve these goals and the successfulness of home schooling can rightly be determined by how well parents accomplish these goals.

HOME SCHOOL PROFITS

As the aforementioned research demonstrates, the reasons people home school are many and varied, one blog I encountered was entitled 50 Reasons People Home School. Analyzing all of those would require many pages but the reasons listed in the various studies above can be put into three broad categories: (1) academics, (2) values, morals, and religious, and (3) student safety. This is not to deny that there are other goals but these three categories cover many of the stated reasons and appear in some form on every list.

Academics: What Does Better Mean?

In numerous studies (Basham, Merrifield, and Hepburn, 2007; Ray, 2004; Bauman, 2002; National Household Education Surveys 1996 and 1999) home schooling parents report that they believe they can provide a better education than the public-school system. This is the area that most examine as proof positive that home schooling works, the assumption being that other reasons may exist but student learning is the make-or-break metric. However, there are problems with this metric. As objective as measuring this goal may sound, it is not. The most significant variable is that the term "better," as previously discussed, is not clearly defined in most of these surveys and means many different things to different people. Unpacking the terms a bit more we can see that better may mean a deeper knowledge as may be represented by superior test performance or it may mean broader knowledge such as studying a wide array of subjects not taught in school or it may mean developing a specialization or it may mean something else entirely. In addition to the vagueness of the term "better," a more precise definition would be hard to measure. Not all home school families participate in testing and surveys and a certain amount of self-selection occurs when such opportunities arise whereas public-school students are required to test which of course skews data and results.

The caveats notwithstanding, better academic performance is, in some sense, the profit education entrepreneurs seek and there are some measures available and the general conclusion is that home school students perform as well or better than public-school students on an array of measures and compare reasonably well to private-school students. Some critics argue that comparing home school students to all public-school students is not proper and that they should only compare home school students in the public school that have active parents. They have a point. Some measures do compare college-bound students from both groups as one like-to-like comparison, but such a criticism also makes the larger point about home school families being high investors seeking a better return, after all a key part of the argument is that home schoolers are different and the opportunities for like-to-like comparisons are few.

Academics: Some Data

There are many ways to measure academic success: college admissions, college performance, job performance, self-reporting of home school graduates, standardized testing, and more. We have some data on some of these measures and when they are considered in their totality a picture emerges of a group of students who are performing at least equal to their public-school counterparts and in many cases exceeding them.

The first large sample study on the question of home school academic performance was by Rudner in 1998. Rudner studied 20,760 students in 11,930 families from all grade levels. He administered one of two tests to these students, depending on grade level and a questionnaire to the parents of each family and found that "The achievement test scores of this group of home school students are exceptionally high—the median scores were typically in the 70th to 80th percentile; 25 percent of homeschool students are enrolled in one or more grade levels above their age-level public and private school peers."[54] He went on to conclude that "Home school student achievement test scores are exceptionally high . . . well above those of public and Catholic/private school students."[55] As the table from that study shows, reproduced here as table 5.2, except for math, home school students' perform well above the 50th percentile of private-school students throughout the entire school career and even in math they do not fall below the 53rd percentile.[56]

Some claim the Rudner study was flawed in certain ways: that his data had selection bias and was too white and too Christian and even he expressed caveats about how his research should and should not be used. He said it was suggestive that home schooling could work but not a definitive statement on the matter. I do not want to use the results in a way Rudner himself would not and his results are more pronounced than other studies but the basic findings are consistent with all the other studies on the subject. In a 2004 study, Clive Belfield, professor of economics at Queens College, City University of New York, and the principal economist at the Center for Benefit-Cost Studies in Education, Teachers College, Columbia University, found, and then in 2005 with co-author Levin confirmed, that home school students outperformed public-school students and were performing at the same level as private-school students on the Scholastic Aptitude Test (SAT).[57] In 2001 home school SAT-takers outscored their public-school peers.[58] Belfield examined these results and found that after controlling for various independent variables normally correlated with student performance that home schooler SAT test takers and private-independent school students converge, there is no performance premium over private-school students.[59] Belfield does point out

Table 5.2 Median Scaled Scores of Home School Students (Corresponding Catholic/Private-school Percentile) by Subtest and Grade

Grade	Composite	Reading	Language	Math	Soc. Stud.	Science
1	170 (89)	174 (86)	166 (80)	164 (80)	166 (73)	164 (75)
2	192 (88)	196 (84)	186 (74)	188 (81)	189 (81)	195 (85)
3	207 (74)	210 (74)	195 (55)	204 (71)	205 (69)	214 (80)
4	222 (72)	228 (72)	216 (58)	220 (69)	216 (56)	232 (76)
5	243 (71)	244 (72)	237 (60)	238 (68)	236 (60)	260 (82)
6	261 (71)	258 (71)	256 (58)	254 (65)	265 (72)	273 (77)
7	276 (72)	277 (77)	276 (63)	272 (70)	276 (68)	282 (73)
8	288 (72)	288 (75)	291 (65)	282 (68)	290 (68)	289 (67)
9	292 (63)	294 (70)	297 (61)	281 (56)	297 (63)	292 (59)
10	310 (71)	314 (81)	318 (71)	294 (57)	318 (72)	310 (66)
11	310 (63)	312 (72)	322 (69)	296 (56)	318 (67)	314 (63)
12	326 (74)	328 (81)	332 (71)	300 (53)	334 (74)	331 (72)

Source: Rudner (1999).

that home school students actually slightly under perform, compared to the predicted scores, in the mathematics part of the SAT, but even with control for the independent variables and the slight under performance in math home school students outperform public-school students on the SAT by a statistically significant margin.[60] In short, home school students are performing at the same level as independent private-school students in verbal and outperform all but independent private-school students in math.

Even though Rudner and Belfield were working seven years apart and Rudner's work was subject to caveats that Belfield's was not, they found similar academic results, home school student performance is more on the level of private-school student performance with the exception of math, which may not come as surprise to anyone but was something of a weak spot in an overall strong performance in these studies. Not weak in the sense that the home school performance was below that of public-school students but weak in that it was the lowest score for the home school students.

Surprisingly, there have not been many more studies. Chang, Gould, and Meuse's 2011 study of seventy-four public-school and home school children found that structured home schooling, schooling that involved lesson plans and formal instruction, resulted in the highest academic achievement followed by public-school students and then students in an unstructured home school setting. It is unclear how general these results are but it does demonstrate two points, home school students compare favorably to public-school students but that the comparisons are fraught with problems. Families engaged in unstructured home schooling, what is commonly referred to as unschooling, are not focused on providing anything that looks like a school education or an accomplished test-taker, which is something the researchers themselves encountered when one mother told them: "I think unschoolers by definition will be less inclined to want to participate in an education study."[61]

Professors of education Robert Kunzman and Milton Gaither report in their 2013 survey of the body of home schooling research begin their report by criticizing the Rudner study but then state that the studies they do approve of agree with Rudner's essential findings, without actually saying it:

> there have been several other studies of academic achievement (of home schoolers) prosecuted since the 1980s, most on a much smaller scale. Frost and Morris (1988) found in a study of 74 Illinois home schoolers that, controlling for family background variables, home schoolers scored above average in all subjects but math. Wartes, similarly, found that home schoolers in Washington state scored well above average in reading and vocabulary but slightly below average in math computation (Ray & Wartes, 1991). The HSLDA-sponsored studies also found that home schoolers do comparatively less well in math than in language-based subjects (Ray, 1997a; Rudner, 1999). Likewise, Belfield (2005), in a

well-designed study that controlled for family background variables, found that home schooled seniors taking the SAT scored slightly better than predicted on the SAT verbal and slightly worse on the SAT math. A similar study of ACT mathematics scores likewise found a slight mathematical disadvantage for home schoolers (Quaqish, 2007). Given this persistent corroboration across two decades we might conclude, tentatively, that there may be at least a modest home schooling effect on academic achievement—namely that it tends to improve students' verbal and weaken their math capacities.[62]

A more accurate statement is that every study conducted since the late 1990s has found home schoolers outperform their peers on verbal academic performance in a statistically significant way but not in math where home school academic performance only slightly exceeds their public-school peers. There is no weakening of mathematical capabilities but there is not much improving of them either.

In 2017 Ray reviewed all of the peer-reviewed studies on home schooling academic performance and reported:

> In 11 of the 14 peer-reviewed studies, there was a definite positive effect on achievement for the homeschooled students. One of the 14 studies showed mixed results; that is, some positive and some negative effects were associated with homeschooling. One study revealed no difference between the homeschool and conventional school students, and one study revealed neutral and negative results for homeschooling compared to conventional schooling. Both state-provided data sets showed higher than average academic achievement test scores for the home educated. Most of the studies did not explicitly use or present effect sizes. Effect sizes could be gleaned, however, from 8 of the 14 studies and both of the state datasets, ranging from 0.05 (small) to 1.13 (very large).[63]

There is even less research on other measures of academic success. There is significant antidotal evidence that home school students gain acceptance and do well in college, many colleges and universities have an admissions process for students without traditional transcripts but there needs to be much more research done before any conclusions can be confidently drawn. What can be concluded is that of the studies we have, home school students are matching their public-school peers in performance and according to most studies exceeding it in significant ways. But, the other side of this discussion is that even if home schoolers were merely matching their public-school peers they are doing so at about 10 percent of the cost. Either way the public school is being shown to be much less efficient by producing inferior results at a significantly higher price.

But home school parents are looking at more than academics.

Values and Morals

Besides academic performance parents also want to impart and instill their values in their children. This has been the subject of much criticism with concerns expressed about parents indoctrinating their children and not exposing them to diversity, of course many parents argue that the public-school curriculum is highly politicized and has significant elements of indoctrination in it as well. Most parents do want their children to adopt their values and sense of morality, no parent has the hope that their child will reject everything the parent believes and holds dear.

Two levels of analysis are required to determine if education entrepreneurs are more successful in imparting their values to their children than parents who choose some sort of traditional school.

The first determination is whether non-home schooled children are abandoning their parents' values. I assume that parents, in the main, desire that their children adopt parental values, which can range from religious expression to attitudes toward racial and other diversity characteristics to basic civility and honesty. While we use the term "generation gap" it is probably not accurate to declare that the younger generation has abandoned its elders' values based on some deviations during adolescence. At least some values people hold tend to change with age and changes in life condition.

The larger problem, however, is that the very concept is difficult to define. What exactly constitutes an abandonment of parental values is vague and occupies an immense amount of gray area. For instance, if a child of devoutly Catholic parents becomes a devoutly Presbyterian does that mean that the parents' values were abandoned by this child? At one level, to many, it would. The child has adopted a religious expression that in part emerged as a rebellion to all things Catholic. On the other hand, the child adopted the values of his parents in many other ways: primarily the importance of a Christian-based faith and the desire to be devout in one's faith and more. It is not difficult to formulate all sorts of other scenarios that simultaneously may and may not be an abandonment of parental values.

Even in the face of this difficulty there have been some attempts to measure value differences between generations. Tom Smith of the National Opinion Research Center at the University of Chicago has looked into just such differences in a study called *Changes in the Generation Gap, 1972–1998*. Smith describes his study as follows:

> [T]here are 101 trends covering all three time points (1973, 1985, 1997), plus an additional 52 trends for 1985 and 1997 for a total of 153 trends overall. These have been sub-divided into 20 topics (abortion, civil liberties, confidence in institutions, crime, family, firearms, gender roles, government spending and

88   Chapter 5

taxes, intergroup relations, misanthropy, miscellaneous, politics, religion, sex, sexually-explicit material, socializing, social welfare, suicide and euthanasia, well-being, and work and finance). These 20 topics contain from 2 to 16 variables. his paper uses an across-group, across-time design in which six age groups (18–24, 25–34, 35–44, 45–54, 55–64, 65+) are examined at three time points (1973, 1985, 1997). Generation gap is defined as the difference between the 18-24 age group (the "young") and the 65+ age group (the "old") at each time point. Attention is also given to changes between equivalent age groups at different points in time, but these are not considered generation gaps.[64]

For an example of Smith's presentation, I show in table 5.3 the results of a question about whether abortion should be legal if the unborn child is known to have a birth defect. The results show the support for legal abortions by year and by age bracket.

For this particular issue the eighteen to twenty-four years old age group of 1973 were most supportive (.855) of any group in any year and their presumptive parents, the forty-five to fifty-four years old bracket were slightly less supportive (.812). However, while the age progression does not map to the age brackets perfectly, twenty-four years later when the 1973 eighteen to twenty-four years olds were in their forties in 1997 their support for this issue had actually fallen below (.785 or .790) to that of their parents when they were approximately the same age. Their parents, presumably in the over sixty-five bracket in 1997, were actually more supportive than their children were. Overall, every age bracket in the three sample years supported aborting a child with known birth defects but the details show the difficulty in discussing who abandons whose values. While Smith's data does not perfectly correlate with his sample years as his subject age, it does allow some tracking of how the younger generation's beliefs and attitudes change over time. Smith concluded that there is a persistent generation gap but that in two-thirds of the issues Smith tested intergenerational attitudes converged over time. About a quarter of the issues showed intergenerational divergence but similar trend lines. The different generations moved toward similar viewpoints but at different rates. Only in about 10 percent of the issues were the trend lines moving in opposite directions.[65] This would seem to imply that the younger generation my wander around and experiment a bit but they come home over time.

Smith's findings could imply that home school parents who are motivated by intergenerational values preservation may be overreacting. But there are some other factors to consider. First, even with the convergence that Smith found there is still a significant fifteen-point generation gap, Smith found that while

Table 5.3 Should Abortions Be Legal If the Unborn Has a Birth Defect

	18–24	25–34	35–44	45–54	55–64	65+	N
1973	.855	.855	.853	.812	.779	.761	4,425
1985	.823	.807	.812	.767	.777	.756	2,902
1997	.782	.806	.785	.790	.781	.804	3,652

Note: 1.000 would indicate full agreement.
Source: Smith (2000).

on average the generation gap has narrowed from the 1970s to the 1990s (1973:19.4 percent, 1985:16.7 percent, 1997:15.2 percent), the young are more disconnected from society. They are less likely to read a newspaper, attend church, belong to a religion or a union, or vote for president or identify with a political party ... on all these measures the generation gap increased from 1985 to 1997.[66]

Secondly, home school parents are more alert than others are: it is a key factor that makes them entrepreneurial. They see things differently; they are alert to opportunities or, threats, previously unnoticed. In this case this may mean the parents have discovered a difficulty in passing on their values others do not see or at least do not see as a problem.

Besides some of the issues that Smith found there are other indicators of value transmission problems. Some of these are quantifiable such as this report:

Seven in 10 Protestants ages 18 to 30—both evangelical and mainline—who went to church regularly in high school said they quit attending by age 23, according to the survey by LifeWay Research. And 34 percent of those said they had not returned, even sporadically, by age 30. That means about one in four Protestant young people have left the church.[67]

And, this report on widespread dishonesty among high-school students:

High-school students are not only cheating, lying and stealing more, but they are less ashamed of it than ever.

Of 12,000 students polled by the Josephson Institute of Ethics, 74 percent admitted to cheating on an exam once in the past year. Nearly four in 10 acknowledged stealing from a store during that time, and 93 percent confessed to lying to their parents or relatives.

These are the highest figures since the group started its biennial surveys in 1992.

Researchers were most alarmed by the students' acceptance of their immoral actions.

Nearly half approved of lying occasionally to save money, while 37 percent were willing to lie to land a good job. And virtually all—95 percent—thought they would get away with the dishonesty.[68]

Besides this data, there are attitudes of school officials that give credence to parental concerns. The following excerpt is from a debate printed in a National Education Association (NEA) publication; it does not represent an official NEA position but likely represents the views of a significant number of education professionals. The question debated was: "Is School the Best Place to Teach Tolerance?" Bettie Sing Luke, a multicultural trainer for the Eugene, Oregon, school system argued in the affirmative:

> A resounding yes! on teaching tolerance in school! School is the only common institution where *all* students can be touched and prepared to survive in our society's marvelous and sometimes maddeningly diverse mix.
>
> We are less connected, as a society, than we were when travel and technology opportunities were more limited. Witness the recent instances of school violence, situations that cried out for tolerance.
>
> Schools, I believe, can help redefine "family" and "belonging" and reinforce respect. They have to. It's unrealistic to depend on tolerance being taught at home.
>
> Have you checked the percentages on single-parent and two-job families? Busy parents may have good ideals to pass on to their children, but we are no longer a society of "Dick and Jane" families sitting down for dinner and quality conversation each night.
>
> Nor are all families models of tolerance. Some young people will reject the intolerant attitudes they might see at home, but what about children who are afraid to think beyond what they are told at home?
>
> What if children never hear alternatives to intolerance at home--especially mainstream students, who can go through their entire lives and never be asked to reconsider their positions of privilege.[69]

This attitude undoubtedly concerns a number of parents. The assumption that families are intolerant, incapable of teaching, and need to be redefined is a problem to some. The fights in this battle are many and frequently end up in court; for instance:

> In a lawsuit filed in May 2005 by two groups of parents and citizens, a federal district court issued an injunction prohibiting a Maryland school district from implementing a health curriculum. The court found that the course materials violate the Constitution by attacking the views of certain religions, while

promoting the views of other religions that "are more friendly towards the homosexual lifestyle."

And, in a Kentucky case decided in February (2006), a federal district court ruled that parents don't have the right to have their children opt out of mandatory "student diversity training" designed to stop the harassment of GLBT students.[70]

The examples of how schools must deal with values in conflict could be quite lengthy, indeed, I may have gone too long here, but the point is real and not always measurable in any traditional sense. The ones cited earlier give a flavor of the fact that teachers, administrators, parents, and the courts are involved in trying to resolve these conflicts, almost always to the dissatisfaction of some. Ray found that 73 percent of home school parents cite values transmission as a reason to homeschool.[71]

There is enough hard and soft evidence to support the notion that children do abandon parental values in some measure and that the public-school system has great difficulty in reconciling the values of the various groups they serve. As with education quality and classroom instruction, the public-school system must strive to satisfy the median value set but in a diverse society there are many who are far from the median, the median may not even exist in any meaningful way on some of these issues, the current state of politics show us this to be true. All of these culture and value battles have served as a motivating factor for many families to home school, not just Christian fundamentalists. The values we as people hold may not be universal but the motivation to preserve our values and pass them onto our children seems to be:

> More Muslim Americans are choosing to home school their children, making them one of the fastest growing minority groups within the national home schooling movement.
>
> The value clash between public-school teachings and Islamic beliefs, combined with the dearth of Muslim schools in many communities, leads many of the parents to educate their children independently, proponents of the movement say.
>
> "Muslims prefer a religious-based curriculum as a Christian might," said Fatima Saleem, a South Carolina mother of two who helped create the Palmetto Muslim Homeschool Resource Network, a Web site that helps Muslim families find information on the basics of homeschooling.[72]

It is not just religious home school families who have these motivations. Some African American home school families are concerned for similar reasons:

Many home schooling parents cite reasons particular to their experience as middle-class African Americans, saying they have moved to their nice suburban addresses only to find that both the public and private schools in their area fail to provide black children with strong moral values, a decent education or a sense of African American identity. . . . [O]ther black home schooling parents believe that subjects like history are still taught with too much Eurocentric focus.[73]

If parents prefer that their values be the ones the children adopt as opposed to some alternative value system prevailing at school, then removing the child from the school is a rational choice. Furthermore, this is not a problem of a private school, or even parochial schools will necessarily solve for everyone.

Are Values Being Transmitted?

But, it is not enough to be aware of a problem or opportunity to qualify as an entrepreneur, one must act. Many are aware of these values conflicts, but few actually act but the question remains, are those that do act successful? If they are motivated by values preservation, are they actually achieving their goal?

Ray was interested in this same issue, although almost exclusively from the religious perspective, and he lamented the dearth of real research into this issue:

Parents regularly explain that a primary reason for home educating their children is to ensure that they pass on or transmit a particular set of values, beliefs, and worldview to their children . . . this is true regardless of the general worldview, religious beliefs, or political preferences of the parents . . . researchers should address whether the adults who were home educated are inclined to maintain the worldview of their parents. Almost no research is available on this.[74]

The lack of data on this issue would seem to be attributable to several causes. The nature of the question and its answers, as explained earlier, is vague and often age dependent. And, although the numbers are growing, there are still not many home school graduates and they are not usually centrally located, nor is it costless to identify them. Ray attempted to research this in his 2004 survey and included several questions in his research about religious beliefs of home school graduates and their parents. He found that

In responding to five questions about religious beliefs the participants were asked to consider that every person, whether atheist, Christian, Jewish, or New Age, holds religious beliefs . . . 96% of individual participants reported that their father and mother held basically the same religious beliefs as one another . . . 93% reported that their parents wanted them to hold basically the same religious beliefs as their parents once they were adults and 94% strongly agreed or agreed with the statement, "My religious beliefs are basically the same as those of my parents."[75]

There is much to desire from a researcher's point of view in drawing any dramatic conclusions from these findings. It is only one study and the phrase *basically the same* leaves much room for interpretation and religion is an imperfect proxy for values in many ways. It also fails to measure intensity and adherence to a particular moral code or value set. It is possible to claim to be of the same religion as someone else and share very little in the way of values. Variables such as church membership or cultural norms may be the basis of an answer but do not mean a similar belief system.

These shortcomings, as important as they are, do not negate certain basic conclusions that can be drawn from Ray's research, especially when there is some support from other research. Kunzman found a positive and significant relationship between family cohesion, value transmission, and home schooling.[76] And Ray found that as the children perceive it, their parents were highly successful in transmitting the parent's preferred religious values; 93 percent of parents wanted their children to adopt their religious values and 94 percent of children report that they did. Further research is required, but based on what is available this particular return is being realized.

Value Transmission: Quality Time Matters

Value transmission requires time. Parents and children need to spend time together and it may not be so much that home schooling itself enables values transmission as does the time together. A child attending public school will spend 14,040 hours in the school between the day he starts kindergarten and the day he graduates from high school, assuming perfect attendance and no extracurricular activities. For 2,340 days of the child's formative years, he will spend more awake-time with peers than with parents. Each week during the school year he will spend eighty-five to ninety hours a week either sleeping or in school-related functions, leaving seventy-eight hours for family interaction. Of that time children spend the largest portion consuming media: "The study by the Kaiser Family Foundation shows that children aged two through eighteen spend an average of five and half hours a day 'consuming' media, including two hours and forty-five minutes watching TV. Kids eight and older spend even more time in front of the tube—nearly six and three quarter hours a day."[77] That totals to approximately forty-two hours a week. This leaves thirty-six hours for family/parental interaction, less than the full weekend. If the family is dual income, then the use of professional childcare reduces that number even further. Regardless of other benefits and costs this family arrangement provides, it leaves little time for the transmission of family values between generations which come not from the formal lessons of textbooks but are learned by observation, interaction, and osmosis. The school schedule and the modern lifestyle leave little time for this kind of interaction. Home schooling does.

Child Safety

Parents have a natural and strong desire to keep their children safe. While no environment is completely safe, the public school has become an increasingly dangerous place. Aside from the tragic and well publicized school shootings and all the Covid issues there are regular and more frequent safety issues. Bullying and teasing have always gone on between children, especially between the *in group* and those who are new or different, but in the last couple of decades there seems to be a marked increase in criminal activity and the level of violence in the public school. That is not to say that all public schools are violent or have significant criminal activity, but it is to say that parents are probably right to be concerned and they are:

> In 2018, survey conducted by Phi Delta Kappa International (PDK) found that 34 percent of parents fear for the safety of their children at school. Only five years ago, the number was at 12 percent. This is the highest number of fearful parents that PDK has seen since 1998, when the survey was released in the wake of three tragic school shootings that occurred within months of each another.[78]

Everyday criminal activity has seeped into the school system. The National Center for Education Statistics reports that:

> [In] the 2005–06 school year, an estimated 54.8 million students were enrolled in prekindergarten through grade 12 (U.S. Department of Education 2007). Preliminary data show that among youth ages 5–18, there were 17 school-associated violent deaths from July 1, 2005, through June 30, 2006 (14 homicides and 3 suicides). In 2005, among students ages 12–18, there were about 1.5 million victims of nonfatal crimes at school, including 868,100 thefts and 628,200 violent crimes (simple assault to serious violent crime). There is some evidence that student safety has improved. The victimization rate of students ages 12–18 at school declined between 1992 and 2005. However, violence, theft, drugs, and weapons continue to pose problems in schools. During the 2005–06 school year, 86 percent of public schools reported that at least one violent crime, theft, or other crime occurred at their school. In 2005, 8 percent of students in grades 9–12 reported being threatened or injured with a weapon in the previous 12 months, and 25 percent reported that drugs were made available to them on

school property. In the same year, 28 percent of students ages 12–18 reported having been bullied at school during the previous 6 months.[79]

To add perspective to these figures we can compare them to the crime rates in the general population.

As table 5.4 shows, a public-school student is less likely to be murdered at school but has a significant chance of being robbed and is almost three times more likely to be a victim of a violent crime than a member of the general population. The National Center for Education Statistics reported some other sobering facts as well:

- During the 2017–2018 school year, 80 percent of public-schools recorded that one or more incidents of violence, theft, or other crimes had taken place, amounting to 1.4 million incidents. This translates to a rate of 29 incidents per 1,000 students enrolled in 2017–2018. During the same school year, 47 percent of schools reported one or more incidents of violence, theft, or other crimes to the police, amounting to 422,800 incidents, or 9 incidents per 1,000 students enrolled.
- From July 1, 2016, through June 30, 2017, there were a total of 42 school-associated violent deaths in the United States, which included 28 homicides, 13 suicides, and 1 legal intervention death.[80]

The reality is the total victimization rate reported in 2018 was *higher at school than away from school*.[81] A student was safer on the street than in the school. And this is the good news; "The total victimization rate at school declined from 181 victimizations per 1,000 students in 1992 to 33 victimizations per 1,000 students in 2018—more than an 80 percent decrease."[82] But the total victimization rate away from school declined from 173 victimizations per 1,000 students in 1992 to 16 victimizations per 1,000 students in 2018—more than a 90 percent decrease."[83] So not only are students more likely to be crime victims at school than on the street; crime rates on the street are falling faster than in the school.

The other factor to consider with these statistics is the time difference which makes these statistics even worse. Over the course of a calendar year the student will spend approximately 1,080 hours in school and 7,680 hours away from school. So, when the crime rates in schools are adjusted for the available hours in which a crime can be committed the crime rate increases dramatically.

One example is murder. Using the slightly older but more complete data from 2006 the public schools reported murder rate was .00003 percent, or fourteen for the school year. Since a school year is only 1,080 hours long a more appropriate comparison would be to adjust the figure for a full

Table 5.4 Crime Rates in the Public Schools and the General Population: 2006

Crime	Rate in Schools (%)*	Rate in General Population (%)**
Murder	.00003	.0057
Theft	1.6	2.2
Violent Crimes	1.1	.47

* Based on figures from NCES.
** From http://www.disastercenter.com/crime/uscrime.htm.

8,760-hour year. Would-be criminals in the school have approximately 12 percent of the total time available in a year in which to commit a crime. In the general population, there were 17,034 murders in 2006, or about 2 an hour. In the school system there were 14 murders in 1,080 hours or about 1 every 83 hours. The rate in the general population still dwarfs the rate in the school system but this provides a better framework to compare the two populations. For theft the hourly rate in the general population was 762 per hour and in the school system it was 804 per hour. The hourly violent crime rate in the general population was 162 while it was 582 in the school system. In two of the three measures the school crime rate was significantly higher than the general population crime rate.

These statistics indicate that there is a significant level of violence and criminal activity in the public-school system. These criminals may see the public-school student body as something of a captive audience, a sort of fenced hunting ground. In a way these criminals are entrepreneurs looking for opportunities to commit their crimes when the risk is minimal. However, safety-motivated education entrepreneurs have reacted to this situation and the criminal's plans by removing their children from the hunting ground. If the entrepreneur considers his investment to be primarily in child safety, then pulling the child out of the public-school system is a rational move toward greater safety.

And the Verdict Is . . .

In this chapter I have treated the majority of the goals parents have stated as their reasons for choosing to home school as the sought-after returns on an investment. Even with the gaps in the data, I have shown that many of these goals are being met, that home school students perform very well academically, adopt their parents' values more frequently, and are safer. It could be that with some assumptions and research that this entire enterprise could be monetized and a present value calculation could give "the answer" on the returns to home schooling. That would stretch the data to the breaking point and the answer would probably have a large standard deviation and be almost useless. In many ways the only real test is in the actions of the entrepreneurs themselves—do they persist in home schooling? Only the entrepreneur can decide if the return, the marginal difference between the home school product and the projected public-school product, is worth the investment. Some do abandon the project before graduation but some of those are planned but all entrepreneurship is hard and many do fail. Many home schools do finish through high-school graduation, the latest data shows that almost a third of all home schoolers are high-school students and that it is the largest cohort[84] at the current time and the reverse of earlier trends in the high-school drop-off, demonstrating that an increasing number of home school families are realizing that the investment is producing the desired returns.

NOTES

1. Fryer and Levitt 2005.
2. McKenzie and Staaf, An Economic Theory of Leanring 1970.
3. Flores 2021.
4. Oakley School Board Meeting 2021.
5. Lubienski, Whithger the Common Good? A Critique of Home Schooling 2000, 207.
6. McKenzie and Staaf 1970, 61.
7. United States Census Bureau 2020.
8. The Nation's Report Card 2007.
9. The Nation's Report Card 2007.
10. Coalition for Responsible Home Education 2020.
11. Ray 1997, 74.
12. Weinberg 2007.
13. Graf, Brown and Patten 2019.
14. Munnell and Zhivan, Earnings and Women's Retirement Security 2006, 2.
15. Munnell and Zhivan 2006, 2.
16. Munnell and Zhivan 2006, 5.
17. Coalition for Responsible Home Education 2020.
18. Semega et al. 2019.
19. Moran 2020.
20. Moreno n.d.
21. Hanna 2017.
22. Hetzer 1997.
23. Ray 1997, 28.
24. Coalition for Responsible Home Education 2020.
25. Basham, Merrifield and Hepburn Home Schooling: From the Extreme to the Mainstream 2007.
26. HEDUA: Homeschool Family Profile 2018.
27. Phipps 2004.
28. Bureau of Labor Statistics 2020.

29. Holmquist 2018.
30. Holmquist 2018.
31. Belfield 2004, 22.
32. Time 4 Learning 2018.
33. Phipps, Adding the Costs of Home Schooling 2004.
34. HEDUA: Homeschool Family Profile 2018.
35. U.S. Bureau of Labor Statistics 2007.
36. Compass 2016.
37. Compass 2016.
38. Coalition for Responsible Home Education 2020.
39. HEDUA: Homeschool Family Profile 2018.
40. Federal Reserve Bank of St. Louis 2019.
41. HEDUA: Homeschool Family Profile 2018.
42. HEDUA: Homeschool Family Profile 2018.
43. Axelrod 2019.
44. HEDUA: Homeschool Family Profile 2018.
45. Ray 1997, 48.
46. Ray 1997, 52.
47. Rudner 1999, 6.
48. Ray, Home Educated and Now Adults 2004, 26.
49. Rudner 1999, 6.
50. Kirzner 1973.
51. Mises 1949:1998, 286.
52. Basham, Merrifield and Hepburn 2007.
53. Ray, Home Educated and Now Adults 2004.
54. Rudner 1999, 1.
55. Rudner 1999, 16.
56. Rudner 1999, 17.
57. Belfield 2004.
58. Belfield 2004.
59. Belfield 2005.
60. Belfield 2004, 12.
61. Matin-Chang, Gould and Meuse, The Impact of Schooling on Academic Achievement: Evidence from Homeschool and Traditionally Schooled Students 2011, 201.
62. Kunzman and Gaither Homeschooling: A Comprehensive Survey of Research 2013, 17.
63. B. Ray, A systematic review of the emprical research on selected aspects of homeschooling as a school choice 2017, 611.
64. Smith 2000, 4.
65. Smith 2000, 5.
66. Smith 2000, 14.
67. Desert News 2007.
68. Phan 2011.
69. Sing 2007.

70. National Education Association 2006.
71. Ray, Home Educated and Now Adults 2004.
72. Elliot-Engel 2002.
73. Aizenman 2000.
74. Ray, 2004, 27.
75. Ray, 2004, 6.
76. Kunzman, Homeschooler Socialization 2017, Chaprter 6.
77. MacPherson 1999.
78. School Safety Solutions 2019.
79. This information was compiled from a variety of official sources by The Center for Research on School Safety, School Climate and Classroom Management at Georgia State University.
80. National Center for Education Statistics 2019.
81. National Center for Education Statistics 2019.
82. National Center for Education Statistics 2019.
83. National Center for Education Statistics 2019.
84. Cavanagh 2017.

Chapter 6

Leviathan Grows Restless

In the previous chapter I explored the idea of home school profits and essentially asked and answered how home schooling works. One data point for getting to that answer is how do others react and respond. The education market has responded by offering home school specific supplies and materials, institutions have responded with family days and special programs, but the public-school bureaucracy has responded with resistance and aggression. Why has a movement that has never included more than 4 percent of the student body get such a strong reaction from the system?

Home schooling is an entrepreneurial market-oriented polycentric movement that is successful by many standards. The public-school system is a political-oriented monocentric institution and as a result education entrepreneurs cannot just be market actors but they must be and are political and legal actors as well. To some extent, the state education bureaucracy's reaction is surprising and seems to be an over-reaction given the actual number of people home schooling. There have always been alternatives to the public-school system; private and parochial schools predate the state-financed public-school system not to mention tutors and in-home solutions. So, there is ample precedent for parental choice and abandonment of the public system, but the public system and its constituent groups have fought vigorously against home schooling. This chapter analyzes the political conflict between the home school community and the education bureaucracy as a competition between opposing interest groups. It extends the political analysis of the school system from chapter 2 and examines how home schooling emerged as a significant threat to its position.

THE PUBLIC SCHOOL IS A GOVERNMENT OFFICE

As previously discussed, the local school holds a certain esteemed place in its community. It is one of the pillar institutions of any community and it is easy to forget that it is essentially a branch office of a larger government agency. Almost all, if not all, of its employees are government employees; its hours, location, and services are determined by government officials; and it gets the single largest appropriation in most local budgets and is one of the largest state agencies in most states. As a result, there are large amounts of money associated with the school system at stake in each budget cycle. "Total expenditures for public elementary and secondary schools in the United States in 2016–2017 amounted to $739 billion"[1] or around 4 percent of GDP.

In addition to the total spending on the education system, its largest block of employees, teachers, are well compensated: "Nationwide, the average public-school teacher salary for the 2018-2019 school year was $61,730, according to data from the Department of Education's National Center for Education Statistics,"[2] which is at the national median. But this is the average and half the states pay more, and half pay less with the range being $44,000 in Mississippi to $86,000 in New York.[3] A government benefits package makes the total compensation even higher. Plus, teachers have agreeable schedules, with longer holiday breaks than many jobs, and several months off each year. This is not to say that teaching is easy; it is not and requires many extra hours like most professions. But income is more than monetary compensation and in that area teachers do well. "While the popular view is that teacher pay is relatively low and has not kept up with comparable professions over time, new claims suggest that teachers are actually well compensated when work hours, weeks of work, or benefits packages are taken into account."[4] All of this makes the education establishment and teachers in particular a powerful and well-funded interest group. The teacher's unions enroll have approximately 3 million members who pay over 1 billion dollars in dues each year. The unions have more political operatives than the Democratic and Republican parties combined.[5] This is a perpetual power base "According to EducationNext, the nation's two top teachers' unions have been among the leading financial contributors to national elections since 1990: They have forged an alliance with the Democratic Party, which receives the vast majority of their hard-money campaign contributions as well as in-kind contributions for get-out-the-vote operations." Teachers union members comprise 10 percent of the delegates at the Democratic National Convention, where they represent "the single largest organizational bloc of Democratic Party activists."[6] And they do what every interest group seeks to do: protect their position and improve it if possible, at the expense of others if necessary.

Being completely dependent on government appropriations presents a huge incentive for the school system to be this politically active and despite efforts at reform and a common perception that the public system is declining, the public-school bureaucracy led by the teachers' unions has become a very efficient rent-seeking operation.

The school system is essentially a monopoly that has its position by virtue of government favor. There are private schools and of course home schools but of the 56 million students in the nation 50.7 million attend a public school.[7] The public-school system has two very powerful tools at its disposal for maintaining its monopoly: compulsory attendance and the taxing power of the state. Compulsory school attendance laws are not often challenged and have wide acceptance among the polity so with its foundation for existence secure, the system has been able to make its political investments in other areas.

One of these areas was in erecting and maintaining barriers to entry. The professionalization of teaching has been a goal and a major accomplishment of the school system in general and of the teacher's associations in particular. Every state requires public-school teachers be certified by the state. As with many regulations, this process effectively limits the number of professionals and raises the pay of those in the industry. In most states, a would-be teacher must have a four-year degree from an approved program and then obtain a state certification and then must take continuing credits as a condition of employment. This is a very effective barrier to keeping many from becoming teachers for example most college professors could not teach in the public-school system.

But there are other barriers. A new private school has to comply with many government-imposed rules and regulations. Depending on the state, it may have to be registered, approved, licensed, or accredited. Most states also have regulations concerning the length of the school year and the subjects that must be taught even for private schools. All of these various regulations operate to keep the number of teachers and schools low and make the public system more attractive and the best option for many. The public-school system is a political entity using the political process to achieve its goals but the one overriding goal is securing large budgets. It is from this goal that all other goals flow and any threat to achieving this goal has to be dealt with.

In the quest for budget the public-school system has managed to get its own federal cabinet-level department with the mandated funding that accompanies a federal agency. Over the years, the number of school districts has been dramatically reduced allowing the ever-increasing education budgets to be spent on an ever-shrinking number of schools, and then there is mission creep which also serve its budget goals. The school system expanded its mission and a variety of special programs were legislated into existence that require additional funding such as health clinics, school lunch programs, all-day kindergarten, increasing the mandatory school age, preschool, and after-school programs. These categorical programs, as they are sometimes called, are hard to eliminate and provide significant funds to the school, because after all it is all "for the children."

All of this is explained by rent-seeking and the welfare effects of a monopoly. Monopolies tend to be inefficient, and federal code has several significant laws prohibiting business monopolies because of its negative effects on consumers, yet in one of the most significant things a family ever does, educate its children, they have almost no choice due to the law. Ninety-three percent of children are being educated in a government-run and -protected monopoly. Figure 6.1, which is Professor Gordon Tullock's pioneering model of welfare loss from monopoly, displays these issues graphically.

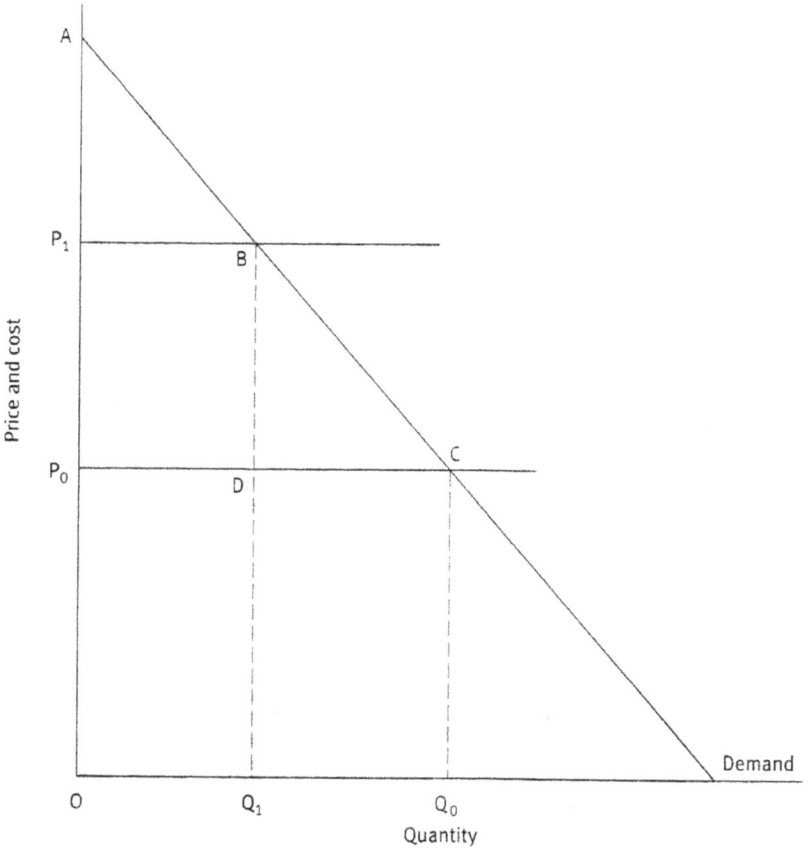

Figure 6.1 Welfare Loss from Monopoly: Tullock Rectangles and Harberger Triangles.
Created by Brian Baugus.

In the figure there are two components to a monopolist's welfare effects. One is the much-discussed deadweight loss, also known as Harberger's Triangle, represented in this graph by points B, D, and C. In the education market this triangle exists because of the barriers that keep school choices to a minimum. This triangle represents schools not getting started which would increase the supply and diversity in the education market and lower prices to students.

The other welfare effect is the monopolist's profit, represented by rectangle P_0P_1BD. In the education market this represents the increasing appropriations, expanded programs, and the general power to tax with public schools getting $12,000 per student per year. When home schooling is educating children and getting better results for under $2,000 a year.[8] Tullock argued that the real cost of monopolies is not the Harberger Triangle of dead weight loss but the resources expended to capture the monopoly profits. An organization will be willing to expend a significant portion of the monopoly profits, primarily in political activity, to preserve its monopoly position. This takes the form of campaign contributions, volunteer time, fund raising, organizational endorsements, and basic electioneering efforts. The more valuable the position the more the monopoly will be willing to expend. That is exactly what we see with a politically protected monopoly, expenditures of significant resources on political activity to protect itself. There are few organizations as politically active and powerful as the teachers' unions.

THE POLITICAL BATTLES

In the early years, almost all the political and legal changes that took place to allow home schooling happened in the courts, the public system had significant influence in the legislatures but the courts were not part of that influence network and the political mood of the country shifted and the changes were remarkably quick "When Ronald Reagan came to power, in 1981, it was illegal for parents to teach their own children in most states."[9] Now, not only is it legal in every state but according to the Home School Legal Defense Association (HSLDA), only six states are considered to be high regulation states with twenty-four being considered low or no regulation states.[10]

Impact of the Reagan Revolution

The political ground shifted in the early 1980s. It pitted two giants of political activism: the public-school bureaucracy, which tends to make its political home in the Democratic Party against the most politically organized subset of home school families, evangelical Christians, "the Religious Right" which tends to make its political home in the Republican Party. The emergence of a strong Republican Party allowed home schooling to challenge the well-connected and politically powerful education establishment and become fully legal in over thirty states between 1983 and 1996. While the differences between Republicans and Democrats may be more marketing and rhetoric than reality at times, the country had displayed a rightward shift in giving Ronald Reagan a landslide victory in the 1980 and again in 1984 presidential election, electing a Republican Senate and a more rightward leaning House. Of course, state elections are very important in education policy and there had been a bumpy but definite trend toward the Republican Party in the state legislatures as well. From the 1974 peak when it controlled thirty-seven state legislatures to 2000, the Democratic Party lost control of twenty-one state legislatures and the Republican Party gained control of fourteen and seven had split party control. Maybe more important than any particular partisan stance is the fact that the political home of the education establishment was out of power and less able (but not unable) to exert itself through its political benefactors. The advance toward ever greater budgets hit a speed bump. The political mood of the country was for a less intrusive government. This rightward shift which seemed to have some momentum for years afterwards if elections are any indicator, combined with some critical reports about America's school systems like *A Nation At Risk* (1983), and a less powerful education establishment favorably prepared the ground for those who might want to challenge the school system. One example of this political shift is "GOPAC, a Republican political action committee [founded in 1978], concluded that school choice was a winning political issue . . . The project was GOPAC's first effort to identify winning issues for Republican candidates."[11]

Meanwhile, at the local level, the public system was taking a strong interest in those seeking to challenge the system and fighting back with legal actions in many cases taking home school parents to court for violation of compulsory attendance or truancy laws. As these attacks continued, home schoolers tried to counter the attacks from what they saw as a predatory state.

Unlike private schools into which the state had extended its regulatory reach, home schoolers were not going to comply with rules that led to an outcome they did not want. They broke with the prevailing education network and began the process of what, in game theory analysis, is essentially an anti-coordination game; the entrepreneurs and the state have opposite goals. One side will only win if the other side loses. There is no compromise or coordination possible between home schools and the public system. The state educational establishment's preferred position is that the home schools not exist at all, but if they did, that they also comply with state rules, essentially turn them into mini public schools. But home schoolers wanted to be free to pursue their enterprises, which was motivated by the desire to leave the state system.

This situation created a tension between what the state feels it is entitled to require and what the home school parents believe are their legitimate rights. Returning to game theory we can analyze this situation succinctly. There is some ambiguity as to which party was the first mover: the entrepreneurs by breaking the established patterns or the state in responding aggressively, but in the analytical calculus it makes little difference. The result is a variation of the hawk-dove game. In a hawk-dove game the two parties compete for a scarce resource and the general form of the payoff matrix is presented here:

In the payoff matrix, V represents the value of the resource and C represents the cost of obtaining and fighting for that resource. If both parties behave as hawks, they will share the net value of the resource (in the above matrix they will share the resource equally as shown in the upper left box). If one party behaves as a dove and the other as a hawk, the hawk wins the entirety of the resource, as shown in the upper right and lower left boxes, and if both are doves they share the total value of the resource, the lower right.

In the conflict between education entrepreneurs and the state, the resource being competed for is really a bundle that consists primarily of rents but also political power and influence, and reputation. The first two are readily apparent, but there is also an intangible, yet real effect that successful entrepreneurs have on the reputation of the public-school system as the only trained professionals capable of producing educated students. This is a real concern for the state system; amateurs producing better students is a clear threat to the stability of the public system.

The issue for the entrepreneurs was that while they were not inclined to be doves, indeed they could not be doves if they wanted to exist, but they did not have the resources to be effective hawks. The state system, with its coercive power and state resources, could increase the cost of fighting beyond what any individual entrepreneur could pay. So, in a case-by-case basis, the hawkish stance of the state could overwhelm even the best-funded and most-aggressive hawkish entrepreneur.

So, in the 1980s, politically minded home school parents formed various organizations to address this situation, to organize home school families and unite them to be able to act more hawkish and match the state resources. The most notable is probably the HSLDA, but there are others. These

Table 6.1 Hawk-Dove Game Payoff Matrix

	Hawk	Dove
Hawk	(V-C)/2, (V-C)/2	V, 0
Dove	0, V	V/2, V/2

organizations emerged as a form of protection from the state and largely emerged from the already-established local home school networks. These new larger organizations work much as the late Harvard political philosopher Robert Nozick describes: "Groups of individuals may form mutual-protection associations: all will answer the call of any member for defense or for the enforcement of his rights. In union there is strength."[12] Nozick seems to imply physical aggression in his formulation but he does not exclude political or legal aggression such as what education entrepreneurs face. Education entrepreneurs have pooled their resources, hired protectors, and put them at the disposal of any aggrieved member of the association. The management of the association is entrusted to address a key problem Nozick identifies: the potential of members to activate the association too frequently. These protective associations are a vehicle for turning this anti-coordination, hawk-dove game between the state and the education entrepreneurs into a coordination game. These organizations are effective by changing the payoffs in the game. They lower the cost to the entrepreneurs of taking a hawk stance and increase the cost to the state of taking a hawk stance. This change can be observed in the way the state's relationship with home school families has changed. In the early years, many of these early confrontations took place in the courts and often involved criminal charges. The state education establishment had some success in getting convictions and undoubtedly scaring other would-be entrepreneurs, but over time as the protective networks emerged the state became less successful in court and attempted those tactics less frequently.

However, the courts are not the only battleground in this conflict and the state had mixed results there anyway. The legislative and executive branches have been involved as well, and this tends to be friendlier political ground for the public education system, which makes the political victories the home school community has won even more impressive. The natural extension of the protective association is the political action group and the next logical step for the political entrepreneurs after court success was to try to influence legislation which also happens to serve the protective association's goal of justifying its continued existence. Thus, the protective association evolved into or spurred the creation of home school special interest groups.

Education Entrepreneurs: A Different Kind of Interest Group

Several exogenous and endogenous factors worked together to allow the home school pressure groups to achieve success. As mentioned previously, the political ground was shifting away from the education establishment. Its very public failings and the electoral losses of its political power base already had the education establishment on defense. The increased discussion and actual implementation in a few places of education choice alternatives had prepared policy makers and voters alike for considering education options.

Despite the public systems' enormous size influence and vast political operations, the home schoolers won some significant victories. Interest group success is a bit counter-intuitive, sometimes small is better. As noted political theorist Mancur Olson explained, special interest groups are most effective if they are (1) small, but look big when they need to, (2) provide significant individual benefits, and (3) provide private benefits.[13] The various home schooling political pressure groups work much like education entrepreneurs themselves work: they form networks as need arises to leverage resources and influence but, at their core, stay small and responsive. Most of them are small compared to the total number of home school families and miniscule when compared to the teachers' union membership. The HSLDA is the largest with 80,000 members. The smaller size also keeps the cost of organizing and the cost of the individual benefits that accrue to members is low. The cost for a family membership in HSLDA is about $100 a year which means that it has an annual budget of approximately $8 million. However, it has regularly defeated the teachers' unions both politically and in court. It has accomplished this by leveraging its networks and members. The HSLDA is ideologically part of the Christian right which includes a variety of organizations with common causes. Being in this network allows HSLDA to expand its influence significantly by tapping into other Christian organizations as well as secular home school friendly networks. Therefore, the Christian home school community was and is able to expand its influence quickly at a relatively low cost. The size of the teachers' unions works against them sometimes creating internal debates about the use of funds and political activity and has made them a bit slow at times. Union leadership must balance a plethora of competing interests and must allocate its resources in such a way that it maintains sufficient support to remain in leadership. The unions look much like the schools with a strong emphasis on process and connections that have hardened over time. The union's very one-sided relationship with the American political system is a prime example. The unions wield significant influence with one party and almost none with the other. The unions have violated Olson's theory that small is better, with size comes significant inflexibility.

In contrast, the small home school groups are nimble. The home school political entrepreneurs build coalitions and form joint ventures; they do not have all the competing interests to contend with and have fewer people to keep satisfied. This is exactly what Olson argued, that every special interest group provides a suboptimal level of the collective good it produces, but "the larger the group, the further it will fall short of providing an optimal amount of a collective good."[14] Therefore the smaller groups are more likely to provide benefits closer to the optimal level. The key to home schooling political success is the same as its academic success; flexibility and networks, and the problem with the teachers' unions is the same as the school system; a politicized inflexible and unresponsive median solution.

Another aspect of home school political pressure groups must also be considered. Even though the Christian right is the most prominent and organized subset of the home schooling community, educational entrepreneurs are a diverse group, and when something threatens one set of home school families it very well may threaten all. This allows pressure to be brought to bear on politicians of all parties and philosophies. The education establishment is so ingrained with one party that their threats of political action against members of the other party carry little real weight. Education entrepreneurs, demonstrating the value of networks over organizations, come in all political flavors and can often exert real pressure across the political spectrum.

Putting It to the Test: A Case Study of H.R. 6

One of the best examples of these two approaches battling for a political victory came in 1994 when the U.S. House of Representatives was considering the five-year renewal of the Elementary and Secondary Education Act, designated H.R. 6 that year. This federally funded program for primary and secondary education must be renewed every five years or it will sunset. As part of the process California Congressman George Miller attached an amendment to H.R. 6 that required all teachers to be licensed in the subject they teach. Its exact wording is as follows:

> § 2124(e). Each State applying for funds under this title shall provide the Secretary with the assurance that after July 1, 1998, it will require each local educational agency within the State to certify that each full-time teacher in schools under the jurisdiction of the agency is certified to teach in the subject area to which he or she is assigned.[15]

The HSLDA determined this amendment had a potentially negative impact on home school parents and alerted its (then) 38,000 members. The intent and actual affect on home schooling can be and was debated by both Congress and the home school community but there was some sense of urgency in acting. HSLDA notified several friendly national networks as well as numerous local home school networks. The reports are that the Congressional switchboard received over 1 million phone calls in the four to five days between the alert going out and the floor vote. The full debate and vote can be found in the Congressional Record of February 24, 1994, but the Miller amendment failed 424 to 1. A substitute amendment was adopted and a second amendment explicitly excluding home schools from the legislation passed with over 370 votes.[16] And so, an amendment supported by the 3-million member teachers' unions that easily passed in committee was soundly defeated on the House floor due to the efforts of a 38,000-person pressure group.

Training Family Lobbyists

Possibly the most interesting program that HSLDA has developed is the family lobbyist program. HSLDA trains willing home school parents as volunteer lobbyists.

> The trainees are taught how to dress . . . field frequently asked questions . . . and access the association's online library and Congressional directory. If they pass muster with the association, the volunteers will be expected to spend four or five days a year on Capitol Hill, meeting each day with seven to 10 staffers for 20 minutes each. That includes children.[17]

Why would anyone choose to do this at a high personal cost? The private benefit entrepreneurs get from this program is that the lobbying is viewed as a teaching opportunity, a civics field trip. Instead of seeing all day spent on Capitol Hill as a day lost, the parents turn it into another node in their education network where the students see government, history, and politics up close. This may sound questionable to some readers, but it is a chance to bring the textbooks and Schoolhouse Rock to life. In interviews with trainees, there is strong evidence that they receive educational and psychological benefits from influencing the process. As one mother put it, "When I started home schooling, I was worried that we were withdrawing from society . . . But now I feel we have the best of both worlds. We home school and we influence education policy nationwide."[18]

It is much cheaper for the association to train hundreds of families to lobby than to have a permanent lobbying presence in the Halls of Congress. *The Wall Street Journal* article quoted earlier mentions that 170 people were attending this volunteer training, if each spends 4 days lobbying a year that is 680 lobbying days or 6,800 meetings with Congressional staffers. The association has effectively transferred the cost of lobbying from the association as an organization to the membership itself. If the marginal cost of acquiring this much lobbying time is the cost of a one-day training seminar then it is a cost-effective operation.

Thinking Nationally but Acting Locally

While the effort and effectiveness of the national pressure groups is impressive, the local political networks do much of the trench work for education entrepreneurs. These emerge, in a micro sense, the same way the larger operations do. While government hawkishness varies from district to district in many cases there is some interaction required between the government and home school families. Education entrepreneurs seeking to avoid or minimize this interaction have developed their own local protective associations. The nature and form of these groups depends upon state and local laws but in general, they serve to keep the local school board and others at a distance by providing an intervening level between the home schools and the government. In some states, home schools must be an affiliate or satellite of a private school, and in those states home schools regularly organize as affiliates of a church school or a private school. In other states, entrepreneurs may form a different kind of protective association called an umbrella. An umbrella is a network of education entrepreneurs who monitor each other in lieu of school board monitoring. Umbrellas often form in states or school districts that have regular school board monitoring. An entrepreneur can join an umbrella whose leaders deal with government officials on behalf of its members, and then have the umbrella members perform the state monitoring requirements for each other. This does not allow the entrepreneur to avoid monitoring but it does allow the entrepreneur to avoid interacting with the local school system officials, which was preferred by many when the state was being more hawkish.

Does EduActivism Work?

So does this fusion of education and activism work? It may be hard to say about the education aspect, although all indicators are in the affirmative, but the activism seems to be successful. "According to the HSLDA, 76 percent of home schooled young people aged eighteen to twenty-four vote in elections compared to 29 percent in that age group in the general population. Home schooled students are significantly more likely to contribute to political campaigns and to work for candidates."[19] Besides making political inroads home school families have also been effective in influencing legislation. They have exerted so much influence that one Congressman called home school lobbyists "the most effective education lobby on Capitol Hill."[20]

The State Changes Tactics

The public success and increased public acceptance of home schooling coupled with the high cost and limited success of legal and political aggression have caused the states' education systems to rethink their approach. There is little to indicate that the professional education and political establishments have changed their views on home schooling: most organizations retain a position that is opposed to home schooling, but they have shifted their tactics. While before, the hawk-dove game was an accurate characterization of the relationship between the education entrepreneurs and the state, it may be more accurate to describe the current relationship as a seduction game. The seduction game is a form of the dictator game where the first mover determines the payoff and the second mover either accepts or rejects the dictator's offer. But unlike the dictator game, in the seduction game the first mover has a strong interest in the second mover's acceptance, and therefore has an incentive not to be a dictator but a seducer.

In this game, the seducer is the first actor and either offers benefits to the target (woos) or does not (shuns). The target then responds by either yielding or resisting. The seducer may increase the offered benefits to a resisting target until the target yields or he may break off the seduction. If the target yields, the seducer gains benefits minus the cost of the seduction. Unsuccessful wooing is not costless but also not expensive. However, the target does not capture the benefits being offered and there is cost to resistance in the form of the opportunity cost of not having the benefits. Table 6.2 presents the payoff matrix of a seduction game.

In the upper left box, the seducer incurs costs but captures benefits, as does the target. In the upper right box, the seducer incurs costs but does not capture no benefits and the target incurs costs to resist the seducer.

In applying the seduction game to the interaction between the state and education entrepreneurs we find that the public schools have gone from fighting home school families in many places to trying to woo them to use the school and its resources in some way. In some districts the public-school system offers home school families supplies and curricula and other support, which, if accepted, allows the public school to claim the student as enrolled in the school, thus increasing their funding.

There are several advantages the seducer has over the hawk. Fighting is expensive and costs must be incurred regardless of winning or losing, but the seducer only incurs significant costs if he wins. The seducer also has better control of his costs. A hawk may fight and incur costs and in the end receive much less benefit than anticipated, but the seducer will woo by offering minimal benefits and only increase them in the face of resistance, but never will increase them above the expected benefit from winning. While it may be difficult to administer, theoretically the seducer will only offer the exact benefits necessary to win and nothing more to each target. Seduction is a cost-minimizing strategy and a rational approach if success is uncertain, as it has become for public-school systems.

The Old Is New Again

Despite forty plus years of co-existing and the successes and uneasy political truce, home schooling is still under attack and misunderstood. Recent examples demonstrate that many people do not know what successful home

Table 6.2 The Seduction Game

Seducer	Target	
	Yields	Resists
Woos	B-C_1, B-C	-C_2, -B
Shuns	0,0	0,0

schooling looks like (hopefully this book will help) and that the education establishment's contempt and distrust of home schooling is not far below the surface.

The involuntary rise in home schooling due to the Covid-19 has opened up the idea of home schooling to many more parents, they may be experiencing that entrepreneurial moment and it has concerned some who are responding by casting serious doubts on home schooling as long-term solution. The recent criticisms are not new and not really accurate and fall into two broad categories; home schooling is bad for the students and parents are not qualified and capable to teach. The second criticism is particularly interesting since many of the critics cannot deny the academic facts established in a previous chapter, as one highly critical paper stated: "it is clear that home schooled students perform well academically—and seemingly outperform their public-school peers,"[21] the authors of this paper just did not accept there was a connection between home schooling and academic performance speculating that "Students who are home schooled would, in all likelihood, achieve at the same academic levels while attending public-school as they do within the home school environment given the amount of parent involvement and higher level of socioeconomic status."[22] In other words high-investing parents produce better students. If you have read this far you know I absolutely agree!

But I do not want to mis-characterize these critics and, while this book is not meant to be a response to critics but an analysis, it would be negligent on my part not to address these criticisms since they are current and lie at the heart of the reason for this book, most people do not understand home schooling or understand how to analyze it.

Harvard Law professor Elizabeth Bartholet made a splash in some circles in the spring of 2020 with her *Arizona Law Review* article "Home Schooling: Parent Rights Absolutism vs. Child Rights to Education & Protection" in which she addressed what she sees as the dangers and failures of home schooling. While this article was published in June 2020, large parts of it sound as if it could have come from some early 1980s, it echoes some of the language in the National Education Association statement on home schooling that was first drafted in the late 1980s and the Colfax children refuted some of these criticisms thirty years ago, yet here we are. However, the arguments are serious and they seem to have staying power.

Professor Bartholet is an articulate presenter of her analysis and conclusions but many of her points are poorly supported with scant data, speculation, and forty-year-old stereotypes. That said, her point should not be ignored, there are bad home schoolers who abuse the system and undoubtedly abuse or neglect their children. That should be dealt with although the professor seems to think that parental transmission of values, especially ones she does not like, qualifies as abuse. True abuse is not unique to home schooling and it seems the professor may be a little over-optimistic to think that enrolling children in a public school solves this problem. As I pointed out the crime rate in the school system is higher than outside it for some crimes. It is telling that the shortest section of her eighty-page article is the little over three pages she spends dismissing (or ignoring) most of the evidence that home schoolers outperform other students. Professor Bartholet's represents a line of thinking and criticism that is very prominent among some and completely ignores the criticisms of the problems with the public-school system. She sees the school system in the most romantic light while seeing home schooling in the worse. Her thoughts can be summarized, in her own words, as follows:

> The nature of the home schooling population presents dangers for children and society. It means that many of the children involved will not be prepared for participation in employment and other productive activities in the mainstream world. It ensures that many will grow up alienated from society, ignorant of views and values different from their parents, and limited in their capacity to choose their own futures. It subjects many to serious health risks.[23]

This sounds old and tired and in the aftermath of Covid-19 the health-risk part sounds particularly out of date. Bartholet is a severe critic of parental rights in general and her home schooling critique is part of a larger project she and some like-minded academics, mostly legal scholars, are undertaking, with the basic point being that home schooling does a disservice to children and is dangerous both to them in the immediate and to all of society in the long-term. She sees all of this danger, despite the findings of shall we say slightly less jaded critics that home school students are high achievers, go to college and get employed at higher rates, are more socially active, and so forth as chronicled in previous chapters. Professor Bartholet represents the schizophrenic nature of the many criticisms: on the one hand, home schooling is detrimental in many ways undertaken by freaks and weirdos, and on the other hand, the public system needs these parents and students involved to be successful. I have dealt with most of her criticisms already and she produces no evidence that abuse rates are higher among home school families but purely speculates they could be.

This leads to the other prevalent criticism, which is based on stereotypes that were never true and assumptions that demonstrate a clear misunderstanding of what is successful home schooling. Professor Jennie Weiner represents this line of thinking. Although an academic, her concerns and critiques are more practical. Writing in *The New York Times* (March 19, 2020), she displays several ongoing misconceptions about home schooling. To be fair, to someone who has not looked at home schooling that carefully and only read a few surface analyses this criticism looks legitimate, but even a few logical questions quickly show the flimsiness of this argument. In the article, Professor Weiner discusses what she observed other mothers doing in response to the Covid-19 mandatory school closures:

> I knew I'd start seeing social media posts with home schooling schedules and amazing and quite labor-intensive (for adults) activities for children. My predictions were right: There have been color-coded home school charts with every minute scheduled, online resources on how to lead children through yoga and meditation, French lessons, and building their own rocket ships. Parents are sharing recipes with the right nutritional balance to enhance study productivity. Many have already begun to lament that they're failing at meeting these new expectations.

She goes on to state that she is "not an expert in teaching third graders, particularly those like one of my sons, who has special needs and receives numerous services from talented professional educators every day to ensure he can thrive. We are so grateful to them and to our other son's teachers and their patience, wisdom, and skill. We know that we don't share these qualities." Then she describes what her family is doing:

> we have embraced the need for some schedule, taking turns keeping an eye on the kids as they surf the internet to make sure whatever they are looking at is age-appropriate. (Of course, one of the boys wanted to learn about bombs.) So far, we've seen them digging into mastodons, dwarf planets, the Mars rover and who made Legos and why. They've been reading a lot (mostly graphic novels and "Big Nate" books) because my kids were always avid readers and I don't have to fight with them to do it. But there are no flash cards and no made-up projects to "enrich" them. We do not assign them essays or ensure their explorations are aligned with Common Core standards. There is no official "movement" or music time. We have not set up a makeshift classroom or given our family's "school" a name.[24]

Professor Weiner's article is simultaneously encouraging and discouraging. Her characterization of home schooling, re-enforced by her (casual) observations of social media commentary displays a certain ignorance about what successful home schooling looks like and that is discouraging that even education professors fall into stereotypes and lazy analysis. As young Grant Colfax observed twenty-five years ago successful home schooling is not replicating the school experience at home. It is not even about enhancing it or doing school better. There are those that do attempt this approach to be sure and almost as many that abandon it quickly; successful home schooling is a completely different approach, a different educational model. Professor Weiner might be quite surprised (maybe she will read this book) to learn that the successful home schools look far more like what she is doing then what she observes others doing or imagines what home schooling is. And that is the encouraging part, she embraced her newfound flexibility and built a customized network, as best she could under Covid rules and allowed a successful home school to emerge and she did not even realize it. As Professor Weiner observes about her own family: "We love each other, we yell, we apologize, we laugh, they punch each other, we yell some more, we make up. We live, we try to be compassionate and we hope this will all be a memory soon. And when it's over, the schoolwork will be there." I would point out that to many home schools this *is* the school work.

Why Attack Home Schooling At All?

The question that underlies all this criticism, and political and legal activity is, why is it necessary? This type of political activity is expensive, so assuming that the people running the public-school system are rational, they and their supporters must see home schooling as a clear and present danger otherwise they would not expend so many resources fighting it. Most interest groups seek their gain at the expense of the larger population; a tariff protects the industry by driving prices up for all. Resistance to this kind of wealth transfer is understandable, even if rare. Home school families seek policies that protect their status, but this is not at a cost to the larger population. If my neighbor chooses to home school he is not imposing any real costs on me. He may be removing some positive externalities if his child has a positive impact on other students but since neither the parent nor the student was being compensated for providing this positive externality it is not accurate to think of his removal as a cost. The tax burden does not increase as a result of home schooling and my neighbor is not capturing any extra benefits at my expense.

However, the public-school system and its political friends are very much against home schooling. Many point to the school funding formula as the reason for this opposition. While the funding varies by state, all state funding formulas include a component for school enrollment: the fewer students in a school the lower the appropriation for that school. While I am not discounting this as a motivating factor for public-school opposition to home schooling, it seems that direct funding concerns are only marginal and only part of the reason for the opposition.

Home schooling is at its historical peak popularity but it is still such a small percentage of the number of students in America that its impact on public-school financing is negligible. The most generous estimates claim that about 2 million students are in home schools, compared to 50 million students in public schools. Two million is not an insignificant number and it represents approximately 4 percent of the total student population in the United States, but it is hard to believe that the funding lost due to home schooling is the make-or-break difference in any school district in the United States.

For nationwide political efforts, 2 million students translates into about $24 billion, not a small sum but all of these actions are at the local level, and do not affect one system disproportionately. Officials in each district must decide if pursuing a home school family, as either a hawk or a seducer, is worth it when the prospect is possibly capturing no more than a few thousand dollars. Local governments have brought a number of cases against home school parents which would seem to be a very expensive way to capture a relatively small cash flow. If the main concern of the local public-school system is lost funds, then it does not seem rational that so much time and resources would be committed to get a few students back into the school.

Therefore, it seems logical to conclude there must be additional reasons for the aggressive opposition from the public-school interest groups. The goal of the education establishment and its choice to use the courts and politics was not retention of a few students, but was motivated by the desire to destroy home schooling as a viable alternative to public schools. These are high-profile tactics meant to draw attention and meant to scare people. Home schooling threatens, in several key ways, the very efficient rent-seeking operation the public-school system has built. Many other forms of school choice reduce public school's enrollment numbers but all of these options are still schools; they do not undermine the school model. Education entrepreneurs' most important threat is they question the school *model* and the very justification for a public-school system's existence. And that had to be met and resisted with all the resources available. It is one thing to have a few private competitors that still have to get through or over the barriers to operate, especially if they are going to operate the same way, they reinforce the model. It is an entirely different situation if any parent can just pull their kids out of school, negatively impacting funding but then use a different approach to produce a better-educated student at a much lower cost. That is an unacceptable threat; the system was not going to roll over and be victims to the Schumpeterian effects of home schooling. Aggressive resistance was essential and when that failed, compromising home schooling with seduction was next but now it is guerilla warfare with attacks here and there continuing. The old guard always resists the entrepreneurs in every way they can. Covid-19 seems to be changing some perspectives on education possibilities and some parents are realizing they are more dissatisfied with the public option than they thought they were. They are opening their eyes to new possibilities such as micro-schools and home schooling.

NOTES

1. National Center for Education Statistics: Fast Facts: Expenditures 2019.
2. Perino, Kiersz and Hoff 2020.
3. Perino, Kiersz and Hoff 2020.
4. Allegretto, Corcoran and Mishel, How Does Teacher Pay Compare 2004.
5. Walberg and Bast, Education and Capitalism 2003.
6. McDonald 2020.
7. National Center for Educational Statistics: Fast Facts: Back to School Statistics 2020.
8. Private School Review 2020.
9. George Bush's Secret Army 2004.
10. George Bush's Secret Army 2004.
11. Lieberman, Public Education: An Autopsy 1993, 109.
12. Nozick, Anarchy, State and Utopia 1974, 12.
13. Olson The Logic of Collective Action 1965.
14. Olson 1965, 48.
15. U.S House of Representatives Bill 6 1994.
16. Congressional Record 1994.
17. George Bush's Secret Army 2004.
18. Golden 2004.
19. Golden 2004.
20. Golden 2004.
21. Brewer and Lubienski, Homeschooling in the United States: Examining the Rationale for Individualizing Education 2017, 27.
22. Brewer and Lubienski 2017, 27.
23. Bartholet, Homeschooling: Parent Rights Absolutism vs. Child Rights to Education & Protection 2020, 14.
24. Weiner 2020.

Chapter 7

So What Happens Next?

The common notion is that home school families are different. That is true in several ways; home schooling started in the subcultures, met with some success, expanded into more mainstream families, and experienced some impressive growth during those years but it seems to have leveled off recently. This is not unexpected and is consistent with the assertion that choosing to home school is an entrepreneurial decision; few people in the population are entrepreneurs.

Earlier I quoted a person from an interview who talked about how home schooling was now being done by normal people, at least from the perspective of the interviewee. Volumes of press articles have been written discussing how home school parents are motivated by having a different worldview or philosophy or religious view from the general population. These easy surface explanations are not wrong but very incomplete and provide no foundation for serious research into explaining why home schooling was and is undertaken by some and not others even within the groups that shared their worldview. These explanations were more of a way to dismiss home schooling rather than understand it. There was, up to this point, no formal theory for why people home school. Much of the serious research I cited examines who home schools, and whether home schooling works, not why they choose to home school.

In this work I offer a comprehensive theory about why those who choose to home school make that choice and how the successful ones operate. Not every home school family is successful but if the family has high dissatisfaction with the public system and the parents are high-investing parents and are alert to the true costs of two-earner families and education procurement, then they are likely to choose to home school. It is the rational logical choice.

It is the option that provides the best return and they have a good chance at success.

Each successful entrepreneur seeking his own self-interest, which is a better educated child, builds a network that provides the customized education he needs. Part of building that network has led entrepreneurs to find each other and thus extend each network and leverage it for maximum value in many ways. This extension has allowed spontaneous markets, the most prominent of which are the co-ops to emerge as well as facilitate the development of protective associations and political action organizations. The result is that an entire order has emerged from the bottom up. This is a complete inversion of the school organization model in which all orders come from the top.

The vital difference between a school system and home schooling is that a school system sets its course and is organized so that the course is followed, while home schooling is an emerging process. Entrepreneurs are seeking to ameliorate dissatisfaction and are continually seeking improvements. There is a sense that a school system has a starting point and finishing point. There is a sense of traveling through a course and reaching a destination. Home schooling is an exploration: there is not a set course or a previously trodden path to follow, and in some sense there is no destination. Paths are ventured down that may lead the parent and student in a whole new direction such as the discovery of a hidden talent or unknown interest, and some paths may be dead ends but that is okay because a home school can pivot in a day.

In a functioning market, an increase in entrepreneurial activity, as has happened in education, would produce reactions such as price wars and product innovations. Schumpetarian mechanisms would create strong pressures to change. This has not happened in the public-school system because the public system is a politically protected monopoly and so it responded with a political response and while it had some victories it lost the war and was not only outmaneuvered in the provision of education quality but also in the political and legal battles.

That brings us to the current situation in which the growth in home schooling seems to have leveled off in the last few years and there appears to be an uneasy political truce between the public system and home schoolers. The teachers' unions still call for it to be highly regulated and for parents to be licensed but have been unwilling or unable to push too hard on that agenda although there is always a little political sniping at the edges. The most recent criticisms are some of the oldest ones that home schooling is cover for indoctrination and child abuse; the evidence for this is non-existent and given that children are at higher risk of crime in the school than outside it, and this does not even consider teacher on student abuse, it seems this is, at best, a weak argument and may verge on seeing things through that romantic lens some see the public schools through.

This has been the situation for a few years then Covid came along creating a huge unknown and shaking that uneasy truce. What parents have seen thanks to the school shutdown is that home schooling can work and some experienced it much differently than what they thought it was. The number of people schooling at home, regardless of how that is defined, has significantly increased; estimates vary but what data we have supports this conclusion. The news that may be most surprising is that a "Back to School Survey Shows 47% of Parents Considering Dropping School, Going to Home schooling."[1] Even if only half this many parents are considering home schooling that is a significantly heightened threat to the public system and if only a portion follows through after Covid there may be some new political battles in the future. The public system had come to terms with the situation and seemed willing to live with the *status quo* but a major disruption to the entire system set off numerous shock waves and reactions that have not fully worked themselves out yet. Only time will tell what will happen next but a crisis can rearrange life in many ways and when children's health and safety are in the mix people will consider all sorts of options.

The experience of home schooling demonstrates the resilience and creativity entrepreneurs have when following their self-interests and seeking to improve their condition. They discover new ways to do things and create value where none existed before. And in pursuing their interests, they can bring changes to all of society. It is the engine of progress and an essential part of our human experience and should be welcomed and encouraged, not resisted and stifled.

NOTE

1. Pecor 2020.

Bibliography

Aizenman, Nurith. 2000. "Black's in Prince George's Join Home-Schooling Trend." *The Washington Post*, October 19.

Allegretto, Sylvia, Sean Corcoran, and Lawrence Mishel. 2004. *How Does Teacher Pay Compare*. Washington, DC: Economic Policy Institute.

Alonso-Cortes, Angel. 2008. "Trade and Language: Adam Smith's Rhetoric of Persuasion." January. https://www.researchgate.net/publication/31513164_Trade_and_language_Adam_Smith's_rhetoric_of_persuasion.

Axelrod, Daniel. 2019. "Tech Needs Drive Up Averae Back-to-School Supply Costs." *The Times-Herald Record*, September 5. https://www.govtech.com/education/Tech-Needs-Drive-Up-Average-Back-to-School-Supply-Costs.html.

Bartholet, Elizabeth. 2020. "Homeschooling: Parent Rights Absolutism vs. Child Rights to Education & Protection." *Arizona Law Review* 62 (1): 1–80.

Basham, Patrick, John Merrifield, and Claudia Hepburn. 2007. *Home Schooling: from the Extrem to the Mainstream, 2nd Edition*. Vancouver: Fraser Institute.

Bauman, Kurt. 2002. "Home Schooling in the United State: Trend and Characteristics." *Education Policy Analysis* 10 (26): 1–21.

Belfield, Clive. 2004. *Home-Schooling in the U.S.* New York: National Center for the Study of Privatization in Education.

Brewer, T. Jameson, and Christopher Lubienski. 2017. "Homeschooling in the United States: Examining the Rationale for Individualizing Education." *Pro-Posições* 28 (2): 21–28.

Brimelow, Peter, and Leslie Spencer. 1993. "The National Extortion Association." *Forbes*, June 7.

Bryant, Jeff. 2020. "Homeschoolers Want You to Believe the Pandemic Has a Silver Lining - They're Wrong." *Salon*. Accessed January 19, 2021. https://www.salon.com/2020/04/11/homeschoolers-want-you-to-believe-the-pandemic-has-a-silver-lining--theyre-wrong_partner/.

Bureau of Labor Statistics. 2020. *American Time US Survey—2019 Results*. Washington, DC: U.S. Deprtment of Labor.

Calvert Education. 2020. *Calvert Education*. Accessed July 10, 2020. https://www.calverteducation.com/calvert-homeschool-experience.

Cavanagh, Sean. 2017. *EDWEEK Market Brief*. November 20. Accessed 2021. https://marketbrief.edweek.org/marketplace-k-12/data-snapshot-nations-homeschoolers/.

Central Intelligence Agency. n.d. "The World FactBook." (C.I.A.). Accessed January 31, 2021. https://www.cia.gov/the-world-factbook/countries/finland/#economy.

Chatham-Carpenter, April. 1994. "Home vs. Public Schoolers: Differing Social Opportunities." *Home School Researcher* 10 (1): 15–24.

Coalition for Responsible Home Education. 2020. *Homeschool Demographics*. Accessed July 2020. https://responsiblehomeschooling.org/research/summaries/homeschool-demographics/.

Coase, Ronald. 1937. "The Nature of the Firm." *Economica* 4 (16): 386–405.

Coase, Ronald. 1960. "The Problem of Social Cost." *The Journal of Law and Economics* 3: 1–44.

Colasanti, Michael. 2007. *StateNotes*. November. Accessed October 2020. https://www.ncsl.org/documents/educ/ECSMinInstructiondays2007.pdf.

Compass. 2016. *Have American Homes Changed much Over the Years? Take A Look*. Compass. Accessed February 2021. https://compasscaliforniablog.com/have-american-homes-changed-much-over-the-years-take-a-look/.

Court of Appeal of the State of California Superior Court. 2008. "Jonathan L. et. al. v. Los Angeles County Department of Children and Family Services et. al." *Court of Appeal of the State of California Superior Court*. JD00773.

Desert News. 2007. "Young Adults Aren't Sticking with Church." *Desert News*, August 7. https://www.deseret.com/2007/8/7/20382133/young-adults-aren-t-sticking-with-church.

Djankov, Simeon, Yigyi Qian, Gerard Roland, and Ekaterina Zhuravskaya. 2007. "What Makes a Successful Entrepreneur? Evidence from Brazil." https://www.researchgate.net/publication/4812533_What_Makes_a_Successful_Entrepreneur_Evidence_from_Brazil.

Elias, Marilyn. 2013. "The School-to-Prison Pipeline." *Learning For Justice*, Spring (43): 38–40.

Elliot-Engel, Amaris. 2002. "More Muslims home in to educate children." *The Washingotn Times*, July 29.

Evans, Dennis. 2003. "Home Is No Place for School." *USA Today*, September 3.

Federal Reserve Bank of St. Louis. 2019. *Real Median Household Income in the United States*. Federal Reserve Bank of St. Louis. https://fred.stlouisfed.org/series/MEHOINUSA672N.

Flores, Jessica. 2021. "East Bay School Board Members Caught on Hot Mic Disparaging Parents." *San Francisco Chronicle*, February 19. https://www.msn.com/en-us/sports/other/east-bay-school-board-members-caught-on-hot-mic-disparaging-parents/ar-BB1dO4xL?ocid=uxbndlbing&fbclid=IwAR3VyUKYE0AYXXdA7aE4PeZSyhANSPhScQSehLNb2-B3rFuYEZJDHm7HAAE.

Fryer, Roland, and Steven Levitt. 2006. "The Black-White Test Score Gap Through Third Grade." *American Law and Economic Review* (Oxford University Press) 8 (2): 249–281.

Gamerman, Ellen. 2008. "What Makes Finnish Kids So Smart." *The Wall Street Journal*, Feb 29.
Gatto, John Taylor. 1991. "I Quit, I Think." *The Wall Street Journal*, July 25.
———. 2005. *Dumbing US Down: The Hibben Curriculum of Compulsory Schooling*. Cabriola Island, BC: New Society Publishers.
Glick-Smith, Judth. 2008. "Succesful Entrepreneurs." *INTERCOM*.
Goff, Karen. 2003. "Learning with Friends." *The Washington Times*, April 27.
Golden, Daniel. 2004. "Home Schoolers Learn to Gain Clout Inside the Beltway." *The Wall Street Journal*, April 24.
Graf, Nikki, Anna Brown, and Eileen Patten. 2019. *The Narrowing, But Persisitent, Gender Gap in Pay*. Washington, DC: Pew Research Center.
Hanna, Kathryn. 2017. *Making Your Money Matter.* May 23. Accessed February 5, 2021. https://www.makingyourmoneymatter.com/how-much-is-a-2nd-income-really-going-to-bring-in/.
Harden, Nathan. 2020. *RealClear Education.* May 29. Accessed July 19, 202. https://www.realcleareducation.com/articles/2020/05/29/covid-19s_surprise_effect_more_parents_are_interested_in_home_schooling_110425.html.
Hayek, Friedrich A. 1945. "The Useof Knowledge in Society." *The American Economic Review* 35 (4): 519–530.
Hetzer, Barbara. 1997. "The Second Income: Is It Worth It?" *Business Week*, August 25. https://www.bloomberg.com/news/articles/1997-08-24/the-second-income-is-it-worth-it.
Hill, Paul. 2000. "How Home Schooling Will Change Public Education." *The Peabody Journal of Education* (Taylor and Francis Ltd.) 75: 20–31.
Holmquist, Annie. 2018. *Intellectual Takeout.* March 12. Accessed February 2021. https://www.intellectualtakeout.org/article/american-parents-spend-6-hours-week-their-kids-homework/.
Home Educating Family Association. 2012. *HEDUA.Com.* Accessed February 2021. https://hedua.com/media-kit/homeschool-demographics/.
———. 2018. *HEDUA: Homeschool Family Profile.* Accessed February 2021. https://hedua.com/media-kit/homeschool-demographics/.
Houston, Robert, and Eugenia Toma. 2003. "Homeschooling: An Alternative School Choice." *Southern Economic Journal* 69 (4): 920–935.
Howley, Craig. 2001. *The Rural School Bus Ride in Five States*. ERIC Clearinghouse on Rural Education and Small School and Ohio University.
Immerwahr, John, and John Jean Johnson. 2005. "What Do People Want from Public Schools?" *USA Today*, July 1.
Jacobs, Jane. 1961. *The Death and Life of Great American Cities*. New York: Random House.
Kirzner, Israel. 1973. *Competition and Entrepreneurship*. Chicago: The University of Chicago Press.
———. 1999. "Creativity and/or Alertness: A Reconsideration of the Schumpeterian Entrepreneur." *Review of Austrian Economics.*
Klein, Dan B. 2005. "The People's Romance: Why People Love Government (as Much as They Do)." *The Independent Review* 10 (1): 5–37.

Kunzman, Robert. 2017. "Homeschooler Socialization." Chap. 6 in *The Wiley Hanbook of Home Education*, edited by Richard Medlin, 135–156. John Wiley and Sons Publishers.

Kunzman, Robert, and Milton Gaither. 2013. "Homeschooling: A Comprehensive Survey of Research." *Other Education* 2 (1): 4–59.

Leary, Timothy. 1983. *Flashbacks*. New York: Putnam and Sons.

Lieberman, Myron. 1993. *Public Education: An Autopsy*. Cambridge, MA: Harvard University Press.

Lines, Patricia. 2000. "Homeschooling Comes of Age." *Public Interest* 140: 74–85.

Lubienski, Chris. 2000. "Whither the Common Good? A Critique of Home Schooling." *Peabody Journal of Education* 75 (1/2): 207–232.

Luke, Bettie Sing. 2007. "Is School the Best Place to Teach Tolerance." *NEA Today*, 18(8): 11.

MacPherson, Karen. 1999. "Kids Spend 38 Hours Weekly Watching, Zapping, Reading." *The Prince George's Post Gazette*, November 18. http://www.post-gazette.com/headlines/19991118kidstv3.asp.

Maraville, Nach. 2000. *PowerHomeBiz*. Accessed February 7, 2021. www.PowerHomeBiz.com/vol14/profile.htm.

Matin-Chang, Sandra Lyn, Odette Noella Gould, and Reanna Meuse. 2011. "The Impact of Schooling on Acadmic Achievement: Evidence from Homeschooled and Traditionally Schooled Students." *Candian Journal of Behavioural Science* 43: 195–202.

Matthews, Jay. 2004. "Correcting Misconceptions About Homeschooling." *The Washington Post*, July 27. https://www.washingtonpost.com/wp-dyn/articles/A17676-2004Jul27.html.

McDonald, Kerry. 2020. "Teachers Unions Are More Powerful That You realize - but That May Be Changing." *Commentary*, August.

McKenzie, Richard, and Robert Staaf. 1974. *An Economic Theory of Learning*. Blacksburg, VA: University Publications.

Meadowcroft, John, and Mark Pennington. 2008. "Bonding and Bridging: Social Capital and the Communitarian Critique of Liberal Markets." *The Review of Austrian Economics* 21: 119–133. doi: 10.1007/s11138-007-0032-2.

Medlin, Richard. 2000. "Home Schooling and the Question of Socialization." *Peabody Journal of Education* 75: 107–123.

Mises, Ludwig von. 1949:1998. *Human Action*. Auburn, AL: The Ludwig von Mises Institute.

Moran, Porsche. 2020. *How Much Is A Stay-at-Home Parent Worth?* March 21. Accessed February 2021. https://www.investopedia.com/financial-edge/0112/how-much-is-a-homemaker-worth.aspx.

Moreno, Tonya. n.d. *Your Guide to State Income Tax rates*. Edited by Janet Berry-Johnson. https://www.thebalance.com/state-income-tax-rates-3193320.

Morris, Dr. Henry, ed. 1995. *The Defender's Study Bible*. Grand Rapids, MI: Word Publishing, Inc.

Munnell, Alicia, and Natalia Zhivan. 2006. "Earnings and Women's Retirement Security." Boston: Center for Retirement Research, Boston College.

Nahm, Nara K. 1989. "Homeschoolers are at Home at Harvard." *The Harvard Crimson*, March 16. http://www.thecrimson.com/article.aspx?ref=132239.

National Center for Education Statistics. n.d. "Fast Facts: Education institutions." (U.S. Department of Education). https://nces.ed.gov/fastfacts/display.asp?id=84.

———. 2010. *Institute for Education Science*. April. Accessed July 2020. https://nces.ed.gov/pubs2010/2010004/findings_10.asp.

———. 2019. *Educational Institutions: Fast Facts*. Accessed July 26, 2020. https://nces.ed.gov/fastfacts/display.asp?id=84.

———. 2019. *National Center for Education Statistics: Fast Facts*. Accessed 2021. https://nces.ed.gov/fastfacts/display.asp?id=49.

———. 2019. *National Center for Education Statistics: Fast Facts: Expenditures*. Accessed 2021. https://nces.ed.gov/fastfacts/display.asp?id=66.

———. 2020. "Homeschooling." *Fast Facts*. Accessed January 2021. https://nces.ed.gov/fastfacts/display.asp?id=91.

———. 2020. *National Center for Educational Statistics: Fast Facts: Back to School Statistics*. August. Accessed 2021. https://nces.ed.gov/fastfacts/display.asp?id=372.

———. 2020. *Private School Enrollment*. May. Accessed July 2020. https://nces.ed.gov/programs/coe/indicator_cgc.asp.

National Education Association. 2006. "Teaching Tolerance or Attacking Religion." *Right's Watch*, May. http://www.nea.org/neatoday/0605/rightswatch.html.

———. 2017. "2016-2017 NEA Resolutions." *2017 NEA Handbook*. 250. Accessed July 10, 2020. https://www.nea.org/assets/docs/Resolutions_2017_NEA_Handbook.pdf.

Newcomb, Amy. 2018. "Women's Earnings Lower in Most Occupations." *The United States Census Bureau*. https://www.census.gov/library/stories/2018/05/gender-pay-gap-in-finance-sales.html.

Nozick, Robert. 1974. *Anarchy, State and Utopia*. New York: Basic Books.

Oakley School Board: Unoffical Minutes. 2021. "Oakley School Board Meeting." Oakley, CA, February 19. https://www.youtube.com/watch?v=C3XaJHU7QlY.

Olson, Mancur. 1965. *The Logic of Collective Action*. Cambridge, MA: Harvard University Press.

Ostrom, Elinor. 2008. "Polycentric Systems as One Approach for Solving Collective-Action Problems." *School of Public Affair And Environmental Affairs: Indiana University* 2–3. https://papers.ssrn.com/sol3/papers.cfm?abstract_id=1304697.

Ozcan, Berkay. 2011. "Only the Lonely?: The Influence of the Spouse on the Transition to Self-employment." *Small Business Economics* 37 (4): 1–50. doi:10.1007/s11187-011-9376-x.

Pecor, Jeff. 2020. *buinsesswire*. July. Accessed February 2021. https://www.businesswire.com/news/home/20200709005777/en/Back-to-School-Survey-Shows-47-of-Parents-Considering-Dropping-School-Going-to-Homeschooling.

Perino, Marissa, Andy Kiersz, and Madison Hoff. 2020. *Business Insider*. August. Accessed February 2021. https://www.businessinsider.com/teacher-salary-in-every-state-2018-4.

Pew Research Center: Social and Demopgraphic Trends. 2015. *Three-in-Ten U.S. Jobs Are Held by the Self Employed and the Workers They Hire*. Pew Research Center. https://www.pewsocialtrends.org/2015/10/22/three-in-ten-u-s-jobs-are-held-by-the-self-employed-and-the-workers-they-hire/.

Phan, Hieu Tran. 2011. "More High School Kids Lie, Cheat, Steal--and Just Shrug." *Scripps Howard News Service*, March 12. https://www.seattlepi.com/national/article/More-high-school-kids-lie-cheat-steal-and-1099093.php.

Phi Delta Kappan. 2018. "The 50th Annual PDK Poll of the Public's Attitudes Towards the Public Schools." Edited by Rafael Heller. *Kappan Magazine* (PDK International) K12.

Phipps, Jennie. 2004. "Adding up The Cost of Home Schooling." *Bank Rate*. November 9. Accessed February 5, 2021. https://www.bankrate.com/finance/personal-finance/cost-of-home-schooling.aspx.

Pollack, Rachel. 2006. "Homeschoolers a Small but Growing Minority." *The Harvard Crimson*, April 17. http://www.thecrimson.com/article.aspx?ref=512786.

———. 2020. *Private School Review*. Accessed February 2021. https://www.privateschoolreview.com/tuition-stats/private-school-cost-by-state.

Putnam, Robert. 2000. *Bowling Alone: The Collapse and Revival of the American Community*. New York: Simon and Schuster.

Ray, Brian. 1997. *Strengths of Their Own*. Salem, OR: National Home Education Research Institute.

———. 2004. *Home Educated and Now Adults*. Salem, Oregon.

———. 2017. "A Systematic Review of the Emprical Research on selected aspects of Homeschooling as a School Choice." *Journal of School Choice* 11 (4): 604–621. doi: 10.1080/15582159.2017.1395638.

Rea, Amy. 2020. *How Serious Is America's Literacy Problem*. April 29. Accessed July 2020. https://www.libraryjournal.com/?detailStory=How-Serious-Is-Americas-Literacy-Problem.

Reynolds, Paul, William Gartner, Patricia Greene, Larry Cox, and Nancy Carter. 2002. "The Entrepreneur Next Door: Characteristics of Individuals Starting Companies in America: An Executive Summary of the Panel Study of Entrepreneurial Dynamics." *SSRN Electronic Journal*. doi: 10.2139/ssrn.1262320.

Richter, Felix. 2019. *How U.S. Family Income Have Grown Since the 1950s*. Statistica. https://www.statista.com/chart/18418/real-mean-and-median-family-income-in-the-us/.

Rose, Lowell C., and Alec M. Gallup. 2007. "The 39th Annual Phi Delta Kappa/Gallup Poll of the Public's Attitudes Toward Public Schools." 33–48, September

Rudner, Lawrence. 1999. *Scholastic Achivement and Demongraphic Characteristics of Home School Students in 1998*. ERIC Clearinghouse on Assessment and Evaluation College Library and Information Services. http://www.responsiblehomeschooling.org/wp-content/uploads/2013/09/Rudner-Scholastic-Acheivement-and-Demographic-Characteristics-of-Home-School-Students-in-1998.pdf.

Sable, Jennifer, and Jason Hill. 2006. "Overview of Public Elementary and Secondary Students, Staff, Schools, School Districts, Revenuew and Expenditures: School

Year 2004-05 and Fiscal Year 2004." *National Center of Educational Statistics.* http://nces.ed.gov/pubs2007/overview04/tables/table_2.asp?referer=list.

Schaeffer, Francis. 1982. "Priorities 1982." *On Education.* L'Abri Ministries. Accessed July 10, 2020. https://www.schaefferstudycenter.org/francis-schaeffer-on-education/.

School Safety Solutions. 2019. *School Safety Solutions.* April 29. Accessed 2021. https://www.schoolsafetysolution.com/are-public-schools-safe-anymore/.

Schumpeter, Joseph A. 1942 (1976). *Capitalis, Socialism and Democracy.* New York: Harper and Row.

Schworn, Peter. 2003. "School Bells in More Homes." *The Boston Globe,* December 28.

Semega, Jessica, Melissa Kollar, John Creamer, and Abinash Mohanty. 2019. *Table A-7: Number and Real Median Earnings of Total Workers and Full-Time, Year-Round Workers by Sex and Female-to-Male Earnings Ratio: 1960 to 2018.* Washington, DC: United States Census Bureau.

Smith, Tom W. 2000. *Changes in the Generation Gap 1972-1998.* Chicago: General Social Survey.

The Economist. 2004. "George Bush's Secret Army." February 26.

The Economist. 2006. "Searching for the Invisible Man." March 9: 68. Accessed September 1, 2020. https://www.economist.com/finance-and-economics/2006/03/09/searching-for-the-invisible-man.

The Editorial Team. 2021. "Crisis Point: The State of Literacy in America." *Resilent Educator.* https://resilienteducator.com/news/illiteracy-in-america/.

The Los Angeles Times. 1953. "Mother Defends Educating Child." February 7: 18.

The Nation's Report Card. 2007. "State Perfomance Compared to the Nation." National Center for Education Statistics, U.S. Department of Education. https://www.nationsreportcard.gov/profiles/stateprofile?chort=2&sub=MAT&sj=DS&sfj=NP&st=MN&year=2007R3.

The New York Times. 1936. "Boy Backs Mother in Education Row." November 3: 27.

Tikkanen, Jenni. 2019. "Parental school satisfaction in the context of segregation of basic education in urban Finland." *Nordic Journal of Studies in Educational Policy,* 4(3): 165–179. doi: 10.1080/20020317.2019.1688451.

Time 4 Learning. 2018. *Time 4 Learning.* January 11. Accessed February 6, 2021. https://www.time4learning.com/blog/new-homeschooler/how-much-does-home-schooling-cost/.

Time. 1978. "Education: Teaching Children at Home." December 4. Accessed October 2020. http://content.time.com/time/magazine/article/0,9171,912280,00.html.

Tucker, Jeffrey. 2015. "Capitlaism Is Love." The Acton Institute, January 29.

Tullock, Gordon. 1967. "The Welfare Costs of Tariffs, Monopolies and Theft." *Western Economic Journal* 5 (3): 224–232.

———. 1981. "Why So Much Stability." *Public Choice* (Martinus Nijhoff) 37 (2): 189–205.

United States Census Bureau. 2020. *U.S. School System Spending Per Pupil by Region.* Washington, DC: U.S. Department of Commerce.

U.S. Bureau of Labor Statistics. 2007. *Changes in Men's and Women's Labor Force Participation Rates*. Wasgington, DC: U.S. Department of Labor.

U.S. Census Bureau. 2002. "Survey of Business Owners - Characteristics of Business Owners 2002." Department of Commerce, Washington, DC

———. 2015. "Los Angeles County a Microcosm of Nation's Diverse Collection of Business Owners." Department of Commerce, Washington, DC

U.S. Department of Education. 2005. *The Condition of Education 2005.* Washington, DC: National Center for Education Statistics.

U.S. Department of Education, National Center for Education Statistics. n.d. "Table 8. Percentage of Students enrolled in grades 3–12 whose parents were satisfied or dissatisfied with various aspects of their children's schools." https://nces.ed.gov/pubs2010/2010004/tables/table_8.asp.

U.S. House of Representatives. 1994. "Congressional Record." February 24.

———. 1994. "U.S House of Representatives Bill 6." *Congressional Record.*

Vanorman, Alicia, and Linda Jacobsen. 2020. *U.S Household Composition Shifts as the Population Grows Older; More Young Adults Live With Parents.* Washington, DC: Population Reference Bureau.

Walberg, Herbert, and Joseph Bast. 2003. *Education and Capitalism.* CA: The Hoover Institution on War, Revolution and Peace.

Walters, Laurel Shaper. 1991. "From Home Instruction to Harvard University." *The Christian Science Monitor*, April 15. Accessed July 2020. https://www.csmonitor.com/1991/0415/d2home.html.

Weinberg, Daniel. 2007. "Earnings by Gender: Evidence from Census 2000." *Monthly Labor Review* 27.

Weiner, Jennie. 2020. "I Refuse to Run a Coronavirus Home School." *The New York Times*, March 19. https://www.nytimes.com/2020/03/19/opinion/coronavirus-home-school.html.

Wikipedia. n.d. Accessed February 9, 2021. https://en.wikipedia.org/wiki/Wikipedia:Statistics.

Index

abuse, 2, 115
academic achievement: as measure of success, 65, 66; as profit, 82–86; and spending per pupil, 70–71, 77
activities: and networks, 51–52, 58; non-instructional, 59
administration, 71
African Americans, 91–92
alertness: and entrepreneurship, 35–37; and home-school families, 39–41, 46, 47; and values, 89
Amish, 5
Arizona Law Review, 114
assault, 94
Astebro, Thomas, 34
Austria, 32

barriers to entry, 103–105, 118
Bartholet, Elizabeth, 115–16
Basham, Patrick, 81–82
basic skills, 17
Bauman, Kurt, 43, 82
Baumol, William, 33–35, 37, 39
Beede, Kim, 69
Belfield, Clive, 84
Bongart family, 1
Brazil, 45–46
Brewer, T. Jameson, 13, 14
Brizendine, Lisa, 69

bullying, 94, 95
bureaucracy, 67–70, 101–105
Bureau of Census, 42
Bureau of Labor Statistics, 76
Business Week, 74

California, 2
capitalism, 32
Capitalism, Socialism and Democracy, 32
certification (of teachers), 2, 103, 110
Changes in the Generation Gap, 1972–1998, 87–88
charter schools, 15, 24, 26
Chatham-Carpenter, April, 58
childcare, 73–74, 76
Christians, 2–5, 105–108
Coalition for Responsible Home Education, 75
Coase, Ronald, 54
Colfax family, 9–10, 114, 117
college success, 86
Columbia University, 84
common good, 69–70
community. *See* society
commute, 59–60
compulsory attendance, 1–2, 5, 16, 103, 104, 106
consolidation, 15

Consumer Population Survey (2000), 42–44
control, 46, 50–52, 67
co-op, 55–56, 77
costs: expenses as, 77–80; income loss as, 71–75; as investments, 66, 70–71, 77–78; shifting of, 78–79; time as, 75–77
Cox School of Business (report on entrepreneurs), 41, 46–47
creative destruction, 32–33, 36, 41–42
culture: and counterculture, 2–4; and subculture, 5
curricula, 77
customization: as advantage, 61–63; and parent investment, 66–70; of schedule, 58–61

Delaware, 59
Democratic Party, 102, 105–8
diversity, 23–27, 90–91
drugs, 94–95
dues, 77

Early Childhood Longitudinal Study, 56
Earnings by Gender: Evidence from Census 2000, 72
Economist, The, 33–34
economists, 31, 34
education: and entrepreneurship, 38, 49; goals of, 65; of parents, 42, 44–45; and public schools, 19–23
EducationNext, 102
Elementary and Secondary Education Act, 110–11
Encyclopedia Britannica, The, 55, 79
Entrepreneur Next Door, The, 44–45
entrepreneurship, 10–11, 15, 31–35; and alertness, 35–37; and creativity, 37–39; and education in Finland, 21, 23; and home schooling, 39–47, 49, 117–19
ethnicity, 44

family lobbyist program, 111
family size, 73
Feather, Peter, 75–76
Finland, 21–23
Fitzsimmons, William, 10
Four Loves, The, 38
Fraser institute, 75
Fryer, Roland, 56, 66
Fulbright Scholarship, 10

Gaither, Milton, 85–86
Gallup, Alec M., 25–28
game theory, 106–8, 112–13
Gatto, John Taylor, 9–10
gender gap, 72
goals, 65, 81–82
GOPAC, 106
government, 11, 62–63, 102–5
grandparents, 47

happiness, 65
Harberger Triangle, 105
Harvard University, 10, 32, 114
Hayek, Friedrich, A., 53
Heard Museum, 60–61
Hepburn, Claudia, 81–82
hippies, 2–4; as subculture, 5
Holt, John, 49–50
Home Educating Family Association (HEDUA), 52–54, 75, 77, 79
Home Education Development Association (HEDDA), 56
Home Schooling for Excellence, 9
Home School Legal Defense Association (HSLDA), 105, 107, 109–12
homicide, 94–96
Hunter, Isaac, 35

immigration, 5, 23
income: loss of, 71–75; of teachers, 102
Indiana University, 37
information, 8
infrastructure, 71

innovation, 23, 40–41
interest groups, 16–18, 28, 108–10
internet, 53–55, 79
investment: cost analysis of, 70–78; in home schooling, 66–70

Jacobs, Jane, 6
Jews, 5
Josephson Institute of Ethics, 89

Kaiser Family Foundation, 93
Kentucky, 91
Kirzner, Israel, 35–37, 39, 52; on cost changes, 55, 78; on profits, 80–81; on resource coordination, 58
Klein, Dan, 28
Knight, Alicia, 39–41
Kunzman, Robert, 85–86, 93

labor force participation rates, 72–73
law, 1–4, 16, 27, 103, 105–108, 110–11
Leary, Timothy, 3
leisure time, 75–76
Levitt, Steven, 56, 66
Lewis, C. S., 38
libraries, 57–58, 60
LifeWay Research, 89
Lines, Patricia, 43
living standards, 78–79
love, 38–39
Luke, Bettie Sing, 90

magnet schools, 15, 24, 26
marital status, 42, 43, 72–75
markets: and entrepreneurship, 32–33, 35–36; for home-school materials, 79; and networks, 54–56
Maryland, 90–91
Massachusetts, 70
math, 84, 85
McCardel, Nancy, 74
McKenzie, Richard, 67
Medlin, Richard, 51
Merrifield, John, 81–82

Miller, George, 110
Minnesota, 77
Mises, Ludwig von, 81
monopoly, 103–105
Montana, 70
morals, 87–94
mothers, 72–75
Munnell, Alicia, 72–73
museums, 57–58, 60
Muslims, 91

National Center for Education Statistics, 1–2, 43, 75, 94–95
National Education Association (NEA), 2, 90
National Education Surveys Program, 25
National Household Education Survey, 43
National Opinion Research Center, 87
National Retail Federation, 79
Nation at Risk, A, 106
networks: and academic achievement, 56–61; advantages of, 49–52; emergence of, 52–55; and markets, 54–56, 79; and political activism, 109–10; for protection, 111–12
New Hampshire, 70
New Jersey, 59, 70
New York, 70–71
New York Times, The, 116
New York University, 33, 35
Nixon, Richard, 3
Nozick, Robert, 108

Oakley Unified Elementary School District, 68–69
Obama, Barack, 10
Olson, Mancur, 109–10
opportunity, 35–36, 59–63; costs of, 71, 75–77, 113; as motives, 81–82
Organization for Economic Cooperation and Development, 21
Ostrom, Elinor, 37–38

Ostrom, Vincent, 37

parents: dissatisfaction of, 23–27; as entrepreneurs, 39–47; as interest group, 17, 18; as investors, 66–70; values of, 87–94
parent-teacher associations (PTA), 5, 66
People's Romance, The, 28
Pew Research Center, 72
political activism, 102–103, 105–12
political economy, 32
polycentricity, 37–38
prayer, 3
Princeton University, 33
private schools, 15, 26
profit: academic achievement as, 82–86; analysis of, 80–82; and child safety, 94–96; and entrepreneurship, 31; transmission of values as, 86–94
Protestantism, 45–46
psychology, 33–36
public policy, 19–23
public-school system, 1, 7–8, 101, 117–19; and child safety, 94–96; criticisms of, 13–16; dissatisfaction with, 23–27; and education policy, 19–23; inefficiency of, 70–71, 86; and innovation, 40–41, 61–63; and interest groups, 16–18; as monopoly, 102–8; romantic view of, 27–29; spending per pupil in, 70–71, 77
Putnam, Robert, 6

race, 44
Ray, Brian, 51, 75, 82; on academic achievement, 56–57, 86; on families, 43–47; on home-school participation rates, 80; on transmission of values, 91, 92
Reagan, Ronald, 3, 105, 106
religion, 45–46, 90–91. *See also particular religions*
Religious Right, 105–109
rent-seeking, 102–103, 118
Republican Party, 105–108

Rose, Lowell C., 25–28
Rudner, Lawrence, 43, 80, 83
Rushdoony, R. J., 3

safety, 94–96
Salary.com, 73
satisfaction, 65
Schaeffer, Francis, 3–4
schedule: and costs, 75–77; flexibility of, 57–61
Scherer, Frederic, 34
Scholastic Aptitude Test (SAT), 84
school choice, 15, 26, 108–109; in Finland, 23; and GOPAC, 106; Solow on, 28; Tullock on, 19–20, 104–105
Schumpeter, Joseph, 32–33, 36, 39
self-employed, 42–47
Shaw, Douglas, 75–76
Smith, Adam, 54
Smith, Tom, 87–88
social capital, 6–8, 47
socialization, 51, 58, 62
society, 5–9
Solow, Robert, 28–29
South Dakota, 70
Southern Methodist University, 42
sports, 5
Staaf, Robert, 67
staff, 71
standardization, 61
status quo bias, 20
suicide, 94

taxes, 5, 11, 16, 71, 73–74, 103
taxpayers, 17, 18
teachers' unions, 2, 109–10; as interest group, 16–18; and rent-seeking, 102–3
Texas, 59, 60
time, 75–77
tolerance, 90–91
truancy laws. *See* compulsory attendance
Tucker, Jeffrey, 38–39

Tullock, Gordon, 19–20, 104–105
tutors, 77

umbrellas, 112
United States Department of Education, 25, 103
University of Chicago, 87
University of Michigan, 10
University of Vienne, 32
unschooling, 85
Utah, 59, 70–71

values, 87–94
Vietnam War, 3
Virginia, 61
vouchers, 26, 28

Waiting for Superman, 14
Wall Street Journal, 111
Wayne-Shapiro, Penny, 8
wealth, 78–79
Weber, Max, 45, 46
Weiner, Jennie, 116–17
welfare effects, 104–105
Why Children Fail, 49
Wienberg, Daniel, 72
work, 73–74
Wyoming, 70

Yale University, 10

Zhivan, Natalia, 72

About the Author

Brian Baugus is an associate professor of economics at Regent University in Virginia Beach, Virginia. He holds a PhD and MA in economics from George Mason University, MBA from Vanderbilt University, and a BA in economics from McDaniel College. He is the author of *A Biblical Path for a Prosperous Society* and several articles in both the popular and academic press. Along with his co-author, he was the 2016–2017 Michael Szenberg Prize winner for most original article published by *The American Economist* in those years. He has lectured on the biblical basis of free-market economics at a number of conferences in sub-Saharan Africa and has an ongoing teaching and consulting relationship with entrepreneurs and think-tank leaders in several nations. He writes on entrepreneurship, policy and government, and poverty and economic development issues. He is married and lives with his wife, three of their children (the oldest has moved on her own), and assorted pets in the Tidewater/Hampton Roads area of Virginia.

www.ingramcontent.com/pod-product-compliance
Lightning Source LLC
Chambersburg PA
CBHW061718300426
44115CB00014B/2743